TABLE OF CONTENTS

ALL GLORY TO GOD/THANK YOU...

God, it didn't feel right doing a dedication page, because how could I dedicate to You what already belongs to You? It felt more appropriate to spend this time giving You all the glory and saying thank You.

Let's start with giving You all the glory:

GOD, It is my absolute pleasure, honor, and caution to be a vessel of Your Good News (The Gospel). You are the Source and Reason for any gift anyone would ever acknowledge me for, which is why I will always say, "All glory to God"! You are the Giver of life and I want to live the rest of my life glorifying You! I could never take any credit for any of this because these are Your words. I am just in awe that you would give me such priceless treasure, wrapped up as words, to convey to people. God, You know that this would've been impossible if You wouldn't have given me the words, strength, diligence, and courage to complete this assignment. No one else deserves Your glory! Therefore, I am merely giving to You what belongs to you, ALL OF THE GLORY!

Now for Thank You:

Father, thank You and thank You for Who You are! I would be nothing without You! I don't know why You would choose me, but thank You! You are the reason for all things… this thing (the book) being one of those things. Thank you for loving me so much that you sent Your Son to die for my sins. Thank You for loving my family and friends exactly the same way. Thank You for being an unbelievably great Father to me and not giving up on me.

Jesus, thank You for giving Your life so that I could discover my life in You! Thank You for being unselfish. Thank You for Your love! Thank You for Your example! Thank You for interceding and advocating for me. Thank You for waiting patiently for me. Thank You for loving even when I didn't love back. Thank You for Your friendship... It's priceless!

Holy Spirit, thank You for not only comforting, but guiding me through this journey called life! Thank You for dwelling in me. Thank You for the power you give! Thank You for the leading and NEVER steering me wrong. Thank You for wanting to continue to help even when I ignore You. Thank You calling the Word back to me as I wrote and leading me to discover God's voice when I didn't know which way to go. Thank You for the whispers of assurance when I often doubted the calling. Thank You for being a GPS and rerouting me when I got off course.

Father, **Jesus (Son)**, **Holy Spirit**, You All are God, Three in One, therefore, I would like to say,

God, I am not only thankful for my life, but also for those connected to me like my children, siblings, parents, family, friends, and loved ones. You put the right people in my life that have been an expression of Your love to me. Hallelujah! I not only thank You for Who You called me to be, but also Who You called them to be as well! I hope I don't ever forget to say thank You and never ever forget to always give You all the glory, honor, and praise for all you have done, are doing, and will do for me and all connected to me! Thank You again, and ALL GLORY TO GOD!

LET ME EXPLAIN...

WARNING! THIS PAGE JUST DESCRIBES MY WRITING STYLE, SO YOU ARE WELCOME TO SKIP IT. HOWEVER, REFER TO IT IF YOU HAVE QUESTIONS DURING OR AFTER READING.

Before we begin, I want to explain some things that you will see throughout the book that might be a little different than most books you have read. You will see chunky paragraphs on purpose and weird capitalization in each chapter, but let me explain. I understand the standard sentence minimum and maximum of a paragraph, but I did not abide by those rules. It was my writing style the entire time and when I thought about caring about what people thought about it, I decided not to… so there's that. Also, the capitalization or the lack thereof… I have a funny way of seeing things, so, I don't capitalize the s in satan or the d in devil. When capitalizing the G in God, it is a sign of personal respect and reverence, so even in writing, I will not give him anything of the sort. I do this with the p in pharisees also, but it's my personal dig. Nothing deep. In addition to showing reference to God, when discussing Him, if not already done in the text or scripture translation, I capitalize the first letter of every noun that describes the Holy Trinity (He, Him, They, Author, etc.). The last thing is that I capitalize the W in Word. I was dating someone and they pointed out how the Word is Jesus, so we should capitalize the W to acknowledge Him. I loved that so ever since then, I've done it. Anywho, we can continue with the regularly scheduled program. I pray you are blessed by it!

PRELUDE (BECAUSE WE NEED ONE)...

RECIPE VS. METHOD

Have you ever noticed a person who has had multiple failed relationships usually end for the same reason? My mom bakes cakes and if you know my mom, then you know I'm not lying when I said her cakes are delicious. She has the recipe for every cake she bakes and she is very meticulous while baking. The older I got, the more I wanted to learn how to bake cakes and in college, my mom finally decided to entertain the idea. Why? I guess my mom knew that I needed to be older to really have one of the most important keys to baking an amazing cake, patience. My mom is very serious about following the exact recipe when it comes to her cakes. When she began to teach me, I remember I wanted to rush through it, but she made me take my time so I wouldn't miss anything. And guess what? My cakes taste great… as long as I followed the recipe.

Whenever I tried making the cakes on my own, I wouldn't always have the same success because I wouldn't always take my time or there would be something I would alter. I'm sure you can imagine that my cakes would have a difference in taste and/or texture than my moms would. This whole concept is going to make more sense soon, but this is why the conversation about following recipes came about. I was talking to my mom earlier this year about recipes and their importance. We also talked about how if you follow them exactly, you will always get the same results… ALWAYS! I told her how it reminded of the scientific method. The only difference is that you have a variable that can change and each time that variable changes there will be a different outcome... ALWAYS! Hebrews 13:8, ***"Jesus Christ is the same yesterday and today and forever."*** There was no way for anyone to get variance with Jesus because if He remains the same, the results will be the same.

Throughout Jesus' life, He was the example for how we should be in every relationship we have. I believe the way Jesus lived His life, in each relationship, are recipes for our relationships with others. Matthew 11:29 says, ***"Take My yoke upon you, and learn of Me; for I am meek and lowly in heart: and ye shall find rest unto your souls."*** He told us to learn from Him as in learn the recipe. If we follow His recipe and not change anything, the product will be the same as Jesus had. The reason we fail in our relationships with people is because we take the recipe and apply the scientific method to it. The reason people use the scientific method is because they are trying to determine if something causes a particular outcome or they are trying to improve upon a design by testing a series of variables.

Two things we need to know about the Word of God, number 1, Psalms 33:4 says, ***"For the Word of the Lord is right and true; He is faithful in all He does."*** This means that you don't have to determine the outcome of God's Word by experimenting with other variables because it is true. So, we know that it has the same outcome because Jesus is the Word made flesh and if it says that the Lord is faithful, it means He (Word) does what He says He will. The second thing to know about God's Word is that Proverbs 30:5 says, ***"Every word of God is pure…"***, which means it's flawless, so there is nothing that needs to be corrected. The reason applying the scientific method to a recipe does not work is because the Word of God isn't an experiment. It doesn't need to be tested to determine the outcome because it tells you the outcome. A recipe is the exact same way. It is not meant to be altered or else it wouldn't be a recipe.

A definition of recipe is a set of instructions for preparing a particular dish which is likely to lead to a particular outcome. That means that before I begin there is a set outcome, and if I follow the recipe, I should get that outcome every time. However, the Scientific Method is a process that doesn't initially have a set outcome. It uses experimentation to conclude whether or not your hypothesis (prediction) that you made in the beginning is supported or rejected. If we liken God's Word to a recipe, we should follow it exactly if we want the same results. Well I am sure some of you who go rogue when using recipes will ask why we have to be so strict when following a recipe. Well, experimentation means I am changing out variables to see what causes a certain change in my outcome. This means I don't trust the steps I have and want to test to see if something else will give me the same outcome.

This reminds me of different religions who will say they believe in God, but not Jesus Christ. John 14:6 says, ***"Jesus***

saith unto him, I am the Way, the Truth, and the Life: no man cometh unto the Father, but by Me." If His Word says that Jesus is the only way to Christ, not believing in Him is not going to give you the same outcome. Another example of having a recipe, but testing a variable are Christians who tamper with yoga to try to "center themselves" or "find peace". Isaiah 26:3 says, ***"Thou wilt keep him in perfect peace, whose mind is stayed on Thee: because he trusteth in Thee."*** If you trust in Him or keep your mind on Him (KJV translation), then you wouldn't need yoga, right? This means you aren't following His recipe, but instead are doing the scientific method with the recipe, by changing the variable. His recipe is trusting Him, and the result is perfect peace. If you decide to remove His Word and replace it with a variable called yoga why wonder why you got a different outcome?

Undesired results lead to a series of experimentation with different variables, which gives you different results. Now you are more confused and out of whack than you were before. And again, you wonder why. Just using these two examples, we can see the biggest difference between a recipe and the scientific method is that one is consistent and the other has variations. This best describes our relationships that have failed. Instead of using Jesus' recipes for success, we do the scientific method and change the variable and wonder why nothing is working. Instead of taking accountability and responsibility for not strictly following the recipe, we blame everyone, including God, for the outcome. Now isn't that interesting? Why do we do the opposite of what God tells us to do, but then complain that things aren't working according to how the Word (recipe) says they should?

Every promise Jesus gives, there is a recipe for getting those results! The reason why my mom is so serious about following the recipe is because she knows that if you change anything in the slightest, there will be a different outcome for sure! I fell out of love with baking because I wasn't getting the same results as my mom. Instead of me correcting what I was doing wrong, I got frustrated and quit. Why did my mom get the same results every time? She followed the recipe and didn't try to deviate from it! Me, on the other hand, I would keep trying different stuff to fix what was going wrong and when I couldn't get the same outcome, I quit! We get repetition twisted. You can follow both the recipe and the method and if you do them both the exact way as advised, you will get the same results. Good thing, right? Well not necessarily. If you get the desired results of the recipe, that's the goal. However, if the procedures (steps) of your method yield undesirable results, and you repeat that, you will continue to get those undesirable results.

This means if you've changed just one thing in the recipe or the scientific method, and you continue to follow those steps, you will be in a cycle of mistakes. Proverbs 26:11, ***"As a dog returns to its vomit, so fools repeat their folly."*** You would think after not following the recipe and getting different results, a person would strictly follow the recipe. Unfortunately, that's not always the case. All we have to do is follow the recipe. Jesus told His disciples in John 13:15,

"For I have given you an example, that ye should do as I have done to you." He told them to follow His example. I am sure He said this so that they may get the same outcome as He did. They couldn't blame Jesus for the outcome if they didn't follow His example (recipe). However, when we don't follow the recipe, instead of us taking accountability, we blame the recipe or just flat out quit.

I am going to speak to this in another chapter, but 1 Samuel 15:22 says, ***"...Behold, to obey is better than sacrifice, and to hearken than the fat of rams."*** This is a simple thing that I think we make so difficult. Why do we knowingly disobey, but expect the outcome the recipe promises? I have a better question, why do we do the exact opposite of the Word, but expect the outcome it promises? This is the reason we have so many people walking around with a very skewed reality. Instead of being honest with ourselves and self correcting, we blame everything and everybody else, especially God. The worst part is that we like to blame the recipe when we haven't followed it accordingly. These types of people feel like life is unfair or things are against them, when it's really quite simple. YOU'RE THE PROBLEM, NOT THE RECIPE!

Disclaimer: Before I move forward, I want to point out that this isn't to say that people who strive to do good, and bad things still happen to them, that they aren't following the recipe. Matthew 5:45 says, ***"So that you may be sons of your Father who is in heaven. For He makes His sun rise on the evil and on the good, and sends rain on the just and on the unjust."*** There are instances where people can do things the right way and bad things still can happen (However, God still turns those things for our good according to Romans 8:28). I also want to say that just because you are doing good, doesn't mean you are following God's Word. Just because you are a good person doesn't mean you're going to heaven. That's because there are a lot of good people who have rejected Christ and if He is the Only Way to the Father, that means they aren't getting to the Father. Why? Because a good person who doesn't follow the recipe will not get the desired outcome… simple.

As simple as it is to explain that, it is even more simple to explain how to correct it. All we have to do to get the outcome that is promised, is to follow the recipe. Another way of saying follow the recipe is to say, we must obey. I am going to speak more to the obedience aspect of this later, but the other thing we must do that will help us to get the right outcome is to acknowledge that the results we are getting are our own fault. This is being accountable and responsible for our own actions and not making everyone else responsible for our failures. If we don't learn to recognize that we are the problem and not the recipe, we will never get out of this cycle of failed relationships! This is why we must learn how to first take accountability!

YOU'RE THE PROBLEM, NOT...

ACCOUNTABILITY Chapter 1.

When I first began writing this book, I was recently divorced, therefore I thought it would just be for divorcées. I quickly realized that God wanted to reach a bigger audience. So, the Holy Spirit continued to download different areas where I realized I wasn't following God's recipe. After thinking of almost every area that I could discuss, I noticed that they all had one common denominator, accountability, or the lack thereof. Webster's Dictionary defines accountability as, *"the obligation or willingness to accept responsibility for one's actions."* The reason this is so important is because we miss the opportunity to truly correct an issue that will continue to persist, if left unacknowledged.

Proverbs 28:13 says, ***"Whoever conceals his transgressions will not prosper, but he who confesses and forsakes them will obtain mercy."*** We blame a lot of people or things for failed relationships/ventures and it is unfortunate because a greater majority of our relationships end and ventures fail simply because we never get to the root of the problem. When we cover things up or refuse to uncover/unpack things, it makes it more difficult for any relationship to survive and our ventures succeed, let alone a marriage. The truth of the matter is, we spend more time concerning ourselves with things we can't change about others, which takes up the time we need to be worried about ourselves.

MIRROR, MIRROR

We walk around very proud when we are faced with the mirror. Most of us only own a mirror to look at all of our highlights and hardly ever pay attention to our flaws. The mirror is not just to look at beauty, but it's also used to make us aware of things we may need to correct. Disclaimer: I am in no way encouraging altering your natural features or promoting insecurity. I am simply making a point.

I believe a mirror represents accountability. When I look in the mirror, I can see myself (not just my physical self) and say, *"Here are the things I need to correct in order to be the best person I can be to myself."* We can all do this by asking ourselves, *"Is this the self that I want others to see? Is this the self I want to present to the world? More importantly, is this the self that God created me to be? If not, then what do I need to correct?"* However, for most of us, we do things like cover, mask, tuck, or hide what needs correction, instead of doing the work to correct the issues all together.

As long as you do that, you never have to face the real problem, which is you. Everytime we go to the mirror, what we are saying is, *"As long as I don't see it (because it's been covered), I don't have to accept that I'm the issue."* Here's what's amazing about that. We will hide our issues and walk away from the mirror, only to notice and pick apart the flaws of someone else we have relationships/interactions with. The problem with that is, we present a masked issue to someone and because they didn't cover their flaws, we blame them when things don't go right for us. This causes us to only see the other person as the whole problem and not the added issue. Luke 6:41-42 says, ***"Why do you look at the speck of sawdust in your brother's eye and pay no attention to the plank in your own eye? How can you say to your brother, 'Brother, let me take the speck out of your eye,' when you yourself fail to see the plank in your own eye? You hypocrite, first take the plank out of your eye, and then you will see clearly to remove the speck from your brother's eye."*** This is the attitude of every person in every relationship who has decided that they will blame everyone for their problems. They've gotten so used to covering up their issues that in their mind, they don't exist.

There are two situations that show how people didn't take accountability for their shortcomings and blamed someone else for their problem. Genesis 3:12-13 says, ***"The man said, "The woman You put here with me—she gave me some fruit from the tree, and I ate it." Then the Lord God said to the woman, "What is this you have done?" The woman said, "The serpent deceived me, and I ate."*** And Exodus 32:22-24 says, ***"Do not be angry, my lord," Aaron answered. "You know how prone these people are to evil.***

They said to me, 'Make us gods who will go before us. As for this fellow Moses who brought us up out of Egypt, we don't know what has happened to him.' So I told them, 'Whoever has any gold jewelry, take it off.' Then they gave me the gold, and I threw it into the fire, and out came this calf!" Notice that in both passages, they were asked what they did and all responded with what someone/others did to make them do what they did. Adam, Eve, and Aaron deflected blame, rather than taking responsibility for their own actions. Their response should've been to check themselves to see what would make them make a decision based on what someone else told them, rather than obeying God. This is the very behavior that led me to write this book.

If none of this is true for you, I will use myself as an example. I can remember in a situation I will discuss in more detail later, how I blamed someone for all of the issues. I was so hurt and unforgiving that I had little to no time to self evaluate. Lamentations 3:40 says, ***"Let us examine and probe our ways, And let us return to the Lord."*** I remember being very upset with the person for a couple months after a particular situation happened and I could only see them as the problem. It wasn't until God revealed to me that I had fault in it too, that I began to see things and respond differently. Not only see things differently, but also begin to heal and grow from that place.

We struggle with growing and healing from hurt because we don't ask the hard questions. We also don't like to admit that just like others, we too have faults. Romans 3:23 says,

"For all have sinned, and come short of the glory of God;" All, means everyone, including you! In order for us to get rid of the problem, we have to first admit that there is one to begin with. After that, we have to acknowledge that we are very much responsible and/or a part of that problem. I like to say, *"God can't fix a lie."* As long as we say we aren't the problem, it will never get fixed. However, we can heal if we humbly come to God and say like David did in Psalm 139:23-24, ***"Search me, O God, and know my heart; Try me and know my anxious thoughts; And see if there be any hurtful way in me, And lead me in the everlasting way."*** After I got off my high horse, God began to show me, ME! To be completely honest, I could understand why I didn't want to know I was the problem. I guess because it wasn't the prettiest thing seeing myself in the way God revealed me to me, but it was necessary.

It was almost immediate that I no longer looked at all the things that person needed to do in order for things to get better for me. I had tunnel vision and only looked at what I needed to do better, to be better. From that moment on, I was on a mission to be the best version of myself. At first, it was so I wouldn't be that way I was to someone else in the future. However, the energy behind that shifted soon after. I wanted and desperately needed to be the best version of me for God first and for me second. Not for any motive other than I wanted to be effective for the Kingdom of God. We don't realize that it is prideful to think that we are guiltless at any point and that we don't need God to help us to see what we need to work on. Everything around us is doomed to fail if we allow ourselves to think this way.

Proverbs 16:18 says, ***"Pride goes before destruction, and a haughty spirit before a fall."*** The one relationship I couldn't afford to destroy was the one I had with God. Humility had to kick in quickly because forget any other relationship, me and God's relationship was falling apart!

As much as I knew that my relationship with God needed some work, it was never going to get better if I never acknowledged my wrong. Heck, that relationship couldn't get better if I wasn't better. The only way I could get better was acknowledging my faults because when I didn't, it did more damage than good! Psalms 32:3-5 says, ***"When I kept silent, my bones wasted away through my groaning all day long. For day and night Your hand was heavy on me; my strength was sapped as in the heat of summer. Then I acknowledged my sin to You and did not cover up my iniquity. I said, "I will confess my transgressions to the Lord. And You forgave the guilt of my sin."*** The urgency to take accountability for my actions, helped me get to a place of peace. The anger I was feeling was based on the fact that I couldn't change someone else. I should've been that upset with myself because at least I could control the change that needed to take place in me!

The Holy Spirit revealed to me the other day that we should only focus on what we can change because it keeps us from trying to redirect that focus on anyone else. No matter how much we try, we can't control when a person changes. I could blame people all day long for something, but if I step back and see where I can get better, and change what I have control over, the issue gets at least 50% better. That is way more than 0%! Having this mindset freed me from the expectations and disappointments I had from other people not making the necessary changes to make what "ships" (relationships, friendships, companionships, etc.) work. I knew that if I did the work, I would become a magnet for the right "ships", attracting others who had the same personality.

If I could encourage you all moving forward in this book, I would say that although you are the problem, God has the solution. If you decide today that you're going to read this book and yourself honestly, then you will notice that everyone you have a relationship with (friendship, marriage, family, work, etc.) will begin to either change or organically create the change you want to see! The beginning to solving any problem is to identify it. So let's begin, you're the problem, not…

YOU'RE THE PROBLEM, NOT... GOD Chapter 2

The children of Israel had a real bad habit of not following the recipe and getting upset with God for their failed results. No matter how many times God gave them the most detailed steps to follow, along the way, they decided to change a variable. God wrote out His recipe clear in Exodus 20:3-6, which says, ***"You shall have no other gods before Me. "You shall not make for yourself an image in the form of anything in heaven above or on the earth beneath or in the waters below. You shall not bow down to them or worship them; for I, the Lord your God, am a jealous God, punishing the children for the sin of the parents to the third and fourth generation of those who hate Me, but showing love to a thousand generations of those who love Me and keep My commandments."***

Looking at this verse, I've always assumed that the Israelites never heard this information until after they built the golden calf. I could totally understand if they did something and they didn't know what was expected of them. How could they break a law they are ignorant of, right? Romans 4:15 even says, ***"because the law brings***

wrath. And where there is no law there is no transgression." However we find out in Exodus 24:3&7, that they heard this information well before they made an idol. It says, ***"When Moses went and told the people all the Lord's words and laws, they responded with one voice, "Everything the Lord has said we will do." Moses then wrote down everything the Lord had said. "Then he took the Book of the Covenant and read it to the people. They responded, "We will do everything the Lord has said; we will obey."*** This is a game changer because that means that God gave them the recipe to avoid a failed outcome.

They actually said, ***"... Everything the Lord has said we will do."*** Every time you do a recipe to the exact, you get the desired outcome, and that's what the children of Israel would've gotten. They would've experienced the Promise of Exodus 20:6. Unfortunately, they deviated from the recipe and decided to do the scientific method and test the variable that would ultimately change the desired outcome. Naturally, they did not experience verse 6 of Exodus 20. God told the people He would still give them the promised land, but He wouldn't go with them. So what do you think their response was when they received a different outcome? Exodus 33:4-6 says, ***"When the people heard these distressing words, they began to mourn and no one put on any ornaments. For the Lord had said to Moses, "Tell the Israelites, 'You are a stiff-necked people. If I were to go with you even for a moment, I might destroy you. Now take off your ornaments and I will decide what to do with you.'"***

Why would they mourn if they changed the recipes? Why were they mourning at the outcome, when they knew the recipe and decided to do something different anyway? It doesn't make sense, right? Well, don't be too quick to judge because this is our same behavior when we decide to not follow God's recipes. We get sad or upset and wonder why God is being "mean to us". But is God really the problem? No! I submit to you that if you keep changing the recipe and doing it your own way, you don't have any reason to complain. This is not me being rude, but realistic because at no point in time does God leave us confused. 1 Corinthians 14:55 says, ***"For God is not the author of confusion, but of peace, as in all churches of the saints."*** Confusion comes when there are no instructions.

We can't claim to be confused when He has given us 66 books worth of detailed instructions (recipes) that tell you the outcome. So if He promised you prosperity, He will give you the recipe for it. As a matter of fact, Deuteronomy 28 (verses 1-14) gives you about 14 steps of the recipe for blessings that come IF you follow the recipe. However, He also keeps you in the loop about the outcome of changing the recipe. From verse 15 to 68, God tells Israel all of the outcomes of altering His recipe. God wants us to succeed which is why He gave us the recipe to His blessings and prosperity as well as the outcome if we do the opposite. He doesn't want us to not know and then punish us for being ignorant. No, He gives us what to do, so that we can live an abundant life.

Even if the people around us choose not to obey, we shouldn't look at them as an example. Instead, James 1:22-25 says, ***"Do not merely listen to the Word, and so deceive yourselves. Do what it says. Anyone who listens to the Word but does not do what it says is like someone who looks at his face in a mirror and, after looking at himself, goes away and immediately forgets what he looks like. But whoever looks intently into the perfect law that gives freedom, and continues in it—not forgetting what they have heard, but doing it—they will be blessed in what they do."*** The first thing I want us to stop doing is calling the results of our disobedience, warfare, and blaming the devil for our outcomes! When we think the enemy is coming against us, we will go to extremes to do battle with the enemy, when there is no battle with the enemy to begin with. Most of what we do is self-inflicted and you can fast all day long, but I'm going to keep reminding you of 1 Samuel 15:22, which says, ***"To obey is better than sacrifice, and to heed is better than the fat of rams."*** Why go through all of that when you can just obey?

We also have to stop making ourselves believe that our consequences are a result of a problem that God has and thinking that we can complain to get Him to change His mind. Instead, we must learn to take responsibility for not following the recipe and from there, begin to start over from scratch and follow the recipe. We can't add things to the recipe and start over in the middle of it. We have to start over fresh. Isaiah 43:18-19 says, ***"Remember not the former things, nor consider the things of old. Behold, I am doing a new thing; now it springs forth, do you not***

perceive it? I will make a way in the wilderness and rivers in the desert." Don't hold on to the mistake of messing up, let it go and start over. Go back to the recipe and follow it from there. Every single thing God has ever asked us to do, He has given us the recipe for doing it. Psalms 119:105 says, ***"Thy Word is a lamp unto my feet, and a light unto my path."*** We find His recipe in His Word and that's what we must follow in order to get our desired results!

There is a good example of God giving the recipe and what happens if you don't follow it. God told the priest Samuel to tell king Saul what to do as it pertained to the Amalekites. 1 Samuel 15:3 says, ***"Now go, attack the Amalekites and totally destroy all that belongs to them. Do not spare them; put to death men and women, children and infants, cattle and sheep, camels and donkeys.'"***

<u>Let's look at the recipe that king Saul had to follow in verses 3:</u>

1. NOW GO
2. Attack the Amalekites
3. Totally destroy all that belongs to them
4. Do not spare them
5. Put to death men and women, children and infants, cattle and sheep, camels and donkeys

Now I understand that this is a rather drastic and violent thing that God was asking of Saul, but there was a reason. The Amalekites were evil! They sacrificed their own children to their false gods. On a more personal note, the

Amalekites attacked the Israelites after they crossed the Red Sea, an unprovoked attack, which is why God had reason to deal with them in such a harsh way. Either way, God gave Saul a recipe for a desired outcome that He wanted. Unfortunately, we, like most people who cook, think that if we slightly do something different, it will either make it better or not really mess it up. That is not true at all. Any simple deviation from the recipe will cause something to change, i.e., not come out as desired. And that's our problem! We like to take what God said and tweak it and get upset with the results or with God.

1 Samuel 15:17-19 says, ***"Samuel said, "Although you were once small in your own eyes, did you not become the head of the tribes of Israel? The Lord anointed you king over Israel. And he sent you on a mission, saying, 'Go and completely destroy those wicked people, the Amalekites; wage war against them until you have wiped them out.' Why did you not obey the Lord? Why did you pounce on the plunder and do evil in the eyes of the Lord?"*** Our other problem aside from not taking accountability for our actions, is that in our mind we obeyed God, even though we only did some of what He said to do. Saul's response sounds just like us, in verses 20-21, ***"But I did obey the Lord," Saul said. "I went on the mission the Lord assigned me. I completely destroyed the Amalekites and brought back Agag their king. The soldiers took sheep and cattle from the plunder, the best of what was devoted to God, in order to sacrifice them to the Lord your God at Gilgal."*** In Saul's opinion, not only did

he obey God, but he helped God out by making a wiser decision than God by keeping the best of the spoils.

That one thing he did differently can't be called obedience or a wise decision. You have to call it what it is, rebellion! Samuel told Saul in verse 22-23, ***"But Samuel replied: "Does the Lord delight in burnt offerings and sacrifices as much as in obeying the Lord? To obey is better than sacrifice, and to heed is better than the fat of rams. For rebellion is like the sin of divination, and arrogance like the evil of idolatry. Because you have rejected the word of the Lord, he has rejected you as king."*** The most arrogant thing we could do is think that our way is better than God's or that somehow He made a mistake and we need to help Him fix it. We try to call what we're doing obedience or wisdom, but no matter how you try to spin it as something wise, it's rebellion. God isn't impressed by us not fully obeying Him because partial obedience is still disobedience. So when we don't follow the recipe (obey), whatever comes from that is not what God desired for you, but the results of deviating from the recipe.

Jeremiah 29:11 says, ***"For I know the thoughts that I think toward you, saith the Lord, thoughts of peace, and not of evil, to give you an expected end."*** The first thing we need to fully grasp is that it is or was never God's intent to harm us. The results of rebellion or disobedience will feel like God is trying to punish you, when really those are consequences of a variation. If you do something different than what He said, those results were not God's best for you. We also have to realize God doesn't want us to have some bland life. He doesn't just want us to prosper, but He wants to prosper us! When we deviate from the recipe, we've taken His plans out and inserted our own. As a result, our results look like He abandoned or punished us, when really we abandoned His Word and got the consequences of it.

Contrary to what the enemy would want you to believe, He doesn't want us failing at anything or following directions to only trip us up in the end. Every recipe has what the King James Version of Jeremiah 29:11 calls, ***"… an expected end."*** We have to start taking accountability for our actions and stop telling God we are doing everything He said, when we've only halfway obeyed Him. If we've only done half of what He said, we should stop questioning Him about the different outcomes and realize that WE ARE THE PROBLEM, NOT GOD! Psalms 51:4 says, ***"Against you, you only, have I sinned and done what is evil in your sight; so you are right in your verdict and justified when you judge."*** We have to learn to be honest with ourselves first, because if we don't, we won't be honest with anyone else, especially God. King David didn't cast blame on anyone else when he came to the realization that he had done wrong. As a matter of fact, when he received the consequences of deviating from the recipe, he didn't pout or blame God. He repented!

This is what God wants from us. If we mess up, we should go, talk it out with God, humble yourself and repent of the disobedience/rebellion. Isaiah 1:18-20 says, ***"Come now, let us settle the matter," says the LORD. "Though your***

sins are like scarlet, they shall be as white as snow; though they are red as crimson, they shall be like wool. If you are willing and obedient, you will eat the good things of the land; but if you resist and rebel, you will be devoured by the sword." For the mouth of the LORD has spoken." It's not that God will give the results to you, but the results are due to you following His Word (recipe). You don't have to beg God for it to happen, His Word is just Truth. This means if you obey His Word (recipe), then you get the results of His Truth. We can't do this if we continue to think the same way that we do. We must change our thinking to the way He thinks. Romans 12:2 says, ***"And be not conformed to this world: but be ye transformed by the renewing of your mind, that ye may prove what is that good, and acceptable, and perfect, will of God."***

We renew our minds by getting in His Word (recipe) daily and seeing what and how God wants us to do what He has asked us to do. Although knowing His Word (renewing our mind) is very important, being transformed to being doers of His Word is what makes it most effective. Saul heard what Samuel said God told Him to do, but the problem came in when he didn't execute what He said to do. James 1:22-25 shows us the difference between those who hear the recipe and don't follow it versus the one who hears it and follows it. It says, ***"Do not merely listen to the word, and so deceive yourselves. Do what it says. Anyone who listens to the word but does not do what it says is like someone who looks at his face in a mirror and, after looking at himself, goes away and immediately forgets what he looks like. But whoever looks intently into the***

perfect law that gives freedom, and continues in it—not forgetting what they have heard, but doing it—they will be blessed in what they do." In order for us to get the desired outcome, we must completely follow the recipe and then we will be blessed by what we've done. Doing it and doing it right is so important to the success of the recipe.

Whenever I've ever missed steps that my mom told me to do while baking, I've noticed that the cake falls. It sounds so much like Matthew 7:24-27, which says, ***"Therefore whosoever heareth these sayings of mine, and doeth them, I will liken him unto a wise man, which built his house upon a rock: and the rain descended, and the floods came, and the winds blew, and beat upon that house; and it fell not: for it was founded upon a rock. And every one that heareth these sayings of mine, and doeth them not, shall be likened unto a foolish man, which built his house upon the sand: and the rain descended, and the floods came, and the winds blew, and beat upon that house; and it fell: and great was the fall of it."*** So in order for my cake not to fall, I not only need to do, but make sure that I do what I hear and not do the opposite of what is told for me to do. The same thing is true with us, we must understand that if we fail, it's not because God isn't faithful, but it is because we aren't faithful to the process God gave us.

When we take accountability for our disobedience and begin to follow the recipe, we will not only be blessed as a doer, but we will be all the wiser for it.

Deuteronomy 7:9 says, ***"Know therefore that the LORD thy God, he is God, the faithful God, which keepeth covenant and mercy with them that love him and keep his commandments to a thousand generations;".***

YOU'RE THE PROBLEM, NOT... GOD'S TIMING Chapter 3.

A lot of times when we are following the recipe, we can put in every ingredient, follow the steps correctly, put in the right measurement, and still do one thing differently and get undesired results. The one thing that we do wrong is that we don't follow the instructions of the recipe in regards to time. Some of us don't understand just how important time is and it shows in our results. Some of the reasons we get the results we get is because we try to speed up the process by manually altering the time. Just because you set it to 30 minutes and it really needs 50 minutes, doesn't mean it will be done earlier. Our timing doesn't change anything about what God has said, yet we still try to manipulate it. Psalms 31:15 says, ***"My times are in thy hand…".*** If we acknowledge this as truth, we should understand that whatever time God puts for the recipe, we should respect that and not try to rush it. There are two ways we try to manipulate time, by cutting the time short or by turning up the heat to try to speed up the process.

Increase the Heat, Shorten the Time:

I've noticed that lately my food hasn't turned out the right way, especially my cakes. No matter what I cook, the one commonality is that I cook everything at a higher temperature. When I get "done" cooking, it doesn't look as advertised, nor does it taste like it. For instance, if I bake a cake, and it calls for the heat to be at 350, I turn it up to 450, hoping it will get done sooner. Well, it in fact gets done sooner, but the bottom and the edges are slightly burnt and the cake is hard. Even though I put in all the right ingredients and mixed them well, it still didn't turn out like advertised because I increased the heat. Proverbs 19:2 says, ***"Also, that the soul be without knowledge, it is not good; and he that hasteth with his feet sinneth."*** To sin is to miss the mark. Speeding things up can cause you to miss the mark, especially when cooking. In other words, whenever I am trying to increase the temperature I am trying to make it do something it is not ready to do. It's kind of like when a mother is induced for labor.

We know that there are medical reasons as to why some mother's labor must be induced and it's usually for the safety of both the mom and baby. One of the reasons some moms have long labor, even after being induced, is because you're trying to force the body to do something it's not ready to do. Although it works out, the baby is still coming earlier than desired. Ecclesiastes 3:11, ***"He has made everything beautiful in its time. He has also set eternity in the human heart; yet no one can fathom what God has done from beginning to end."*** When God puts a time on any of His promises, they are coming and if we follow the recipe, they will come out way more beautiful than when we try to rush them out. Applying more heat is baking the cake or cooking the food quicker, but it's not thoroughly getting baked/cooked. As I stated before, the outside and bottom cooks faster, leaving the edges hard and the inside soft or not fully done. That's exactly how we turn out when we rush things. It leaves us hardened on the outside and soft and easily offended on the inside.

Let's look at Sarah. Genesis 16:1-2 says, ***"Now Sarai, Abram's wife, had borne him no children. But she had an Egyptian maidservant named Hagar; so she said to Abram, "The LORD has kept me from having children. Go, sleep with my maidservant; perhaps I can build a family through her." Abram agreed to what Sarai said."*** God told Abraham at the age of 75 that He would give Him a son. It didn't matter how long it would take, if God said it would happen, it was going to happen. Numbers 23:19 says, ***"God is not a man, that he should lie; neither the son of man, that he should repent: hath he said, and shall he not do it? or hath he spoken, and shall he not make it good?"*** Unfortunately, she misinterpreted the length of time as God not fulfilling His promises and that He needed her assistance.

Sidebar: This makes me think of the way the information may have come to Sarah. Scripture doesn't tell us the first time Abraham was told, that Sarah heard or that she even knew. However, we know that she was at the tent door the second time God told Abraham and she heard it then. Same way with Eve,

but these two examples of women being out of order makes it hard for the promises of God to come to pass…

Ok, getting back on track, I totally understand how they intervened. I know from experience how I've doubted the length of time something said it would take to cook. I've even checked it to see if it would get done quicker as if the creator of the dish didn't know what they were talking about. After doing all of that, I still had to wait the time that it said it would cook. Most times when we interfere, we mess things up and that's what Sarah did. She put a rush on God's promise, and after she made that decision, she got undesired results. Genesis 16:4-6 says, ***"He slept with Hagar, and she conceived. When she knew she was pregnant, she began to despise her mistress. Then Sarai said to Abram, "You are responsible for the wrong I am suffering. I put my servant in your arms, and now that she knows she is pregnant, she despises me. May the LORD judge between you and me." "Your servant is in your hands," Abram said. "Do with her whatever you think best." Then Sarai mistreated Hagar; so she fled from her."***

Sarah applied more heat and in the end, she was hardened on the outside, mistreating Hagar, and soft on the inside, sensitive and offended by the decision she made. It was no one else's fault, but her own. Instead of taking responsibility for her impatience, she blamed Abraham and mistreated Hagar. It wasn't fair to Hagar, because she was simply doing what she was told. However, lack of accountability had Sarah imploding and exploding on everyone! I would say it wasn't fair to Abraham either, but at the same time, he knew what God said. Genesis 15:6, ***"Abram believed the Lord, and he credited it to him as righteousness."*** Since Abraham knew what God said, failing to stop Sarah was as if Abraham was co-signing on Sarah "increasing the heat". Length of time isn't indicative of God not being faithful to His promises. God giving us a set time shouldn't be why we believe Him. We should just believe. Habakkuk 2:3 says, ***"For the vision is yet for an appointed time, but at the end it shall speak, and not lie: though it tarry, wait for it; because it will surely come, it will not tarry."***

Although Sarah intervened and took matters into her own hands, God was still faithful to His Word. However, Sarah trying to make something happen that shouldn't have happened at the time, by the wrong means, created more drama than necessary.

Shorten the Time:

Every time I've ever tried to cook something for a shorter amount of time than recommended, it's never fully done. We subconsciously are saying that we don't believe the creator knows what they are talking about. In the case of our life, we are saying, God, the Creator, doesn't know what He is talking about. Shortcuts or cutting corners may seem like the way to take if you want to shorten the time, but some things that cook the fastest aren't the healthiest. You would rather it take whatever time it takes to get the best God has for you, than to rush and get the worst results possible. There is a set time for everything in the earth.

Everything! Ecclesiastes 3:1, ***"There is a time for everything, and a season for every activity under the heavens:"*** Time is only an earthly thing though, because God exists in eternity, outside of time. Which is why when we talk to Him about how long something is, it's not going to make Him urgent enough to change it.

Time is relative to us, not Him. If we say something is too long, for another person it's not long enough, but for God, it's neither because in eternity, time doesn't exist. Since God exists in eternity, outside of time, nothing for Him is too long or too short. 2 Peter 3:8-10 says, ***"But, beloved, be not ignorant of this one thing, that one day is with the Lord as a thousand years, and a thousand years as one day. The Lord is not slack concerning his promise, as some men count slackness; but is longsuffering to us-ward, not willing that any should perish, but that all should come to repentance. But the day of the Lord will come as a thief in the night; in the which the heavens shall pass away with a great noise, and the elements shall melt with fervent heat, the earth also and the works that are therein shall be burned up."*** We have to trust that God's timing is perfect. He is not just doing a work for you, but at the end of it, you will realize that others benefited as well.

Meals that are cooked for multiple people take longer to prepare than a meal that is for just one person. When we rush and things don't turn out well, we get upset with God as if He told us to alter the time something takes. God isn't just giving you the recipe for just you, but He wants everyone to benefit from His promises. Matthew 24:14 says, ***"And this Gospel of the Kingdom shall be preached in all the world for a witness unto all nations; and then shall the end come."*** We have to stop trying to put the same time on a family meal, that we do just for a single person. We can't be selfish just thinking of ourselves. If God set a time, that's the time. Any other time, produces other results than those desired! His promise of salvation, guess what? This world can't end until everyone has been given the opportunity to come into the knowledge of Christ. Matthew 24:34 says, ***"Verily I say unto you, This generation shall not pass, till all these things be fulfilled."*** No matter how you try to rush it, it won't be done until everything has been fulfilled!

Complaining (or overbaking):

I love when you watch the animated version of the story of Moses and they get to the end where it shows the children of Israel after they left Egypt and got across the Red Sea. It seems like it's this happy ending, right? Unfortunately, that's not where the story ends. There is something very interesting about the story. What should've been a happy ending and an even happier beginning, turned into years of lessons learned. The journey to the Promised Land should've only taken 11 days. However, it turned into a 40 year journey in the wilderness. For most people who follow the recipes, what seemed like a long time, if you're patient and see it through, you realize it's not very long at all. However, for those who don't follow the recipe, let's just say the Israelites, what appeared to be long, pales in comparison to how long it actually took them to reach their goal.

Exodus 15:22 says, ***"Then Moses made Israel set out from the Red Sea, and they went into the wilderness of Shur. They went three days in the wilderness and found no water."*** I get it, 3 days in and no water is probably super difficult, but if you only had to wait 8 more days to be where in the land milk and honey flowed, I'm sure it would've been worth the wait! The more they had to wait, the more they complained. It makes me think about every time we open the oven and check it, the more heat escapes and the more time we tack on. Joshua 5:6 says, ***"The Israelites had moved about in the wilderness forty years until all the men who were of military age when they left Egypt had died, since they had not obeyed the LORD. For the LORD had sworn to them that they would not see the land he had solemnly promised their ancestors to give us, a land flowing with milk and honey."*** What sucks is that you do all that waiting, only to not get what you waited for. In some instances, it takes longer because you probably had to start over. You messed it up or you had to put more time on it because it wasn't quite done.

The recipe that Israel decided not to follow was no longer meant for them. After all that waiting, they weren't going to get to enjoy any of it! How unfortunate! Most parents understand this. If you are going to complain about it, then you don't deserve it. Have you ever waited at a restaurant for a long time for a meal? What about waiting at a restaurant for a long time for a meal and instead of waiting for this delicious meal to get done, you left. So not only did you wait a long time, you forfeited the reward of waiting. For the Israelites, not only did they wait a long time, but they waited a long time not to get anything. That sucks! They regretted complaining because when God told them His final decision after all that complaining, it resulted in them getting nothing for their time. Instead of trying to rush God or complaining about the time it takes for His promises to be revealed, we have to be grateful that we are on our way to it. Not only that, but we have to be grateful that it's been prepared for us. The wait becomes a minimal concern when we know that we have a reward to look forward to. God's reward!

Galatians 6:9, ***"Let us not become weary in doing good, for at the proper time we will reap a harvest if we do not give up."***

YOU'RE THE PROBLEM, NOT...

PRAYER Chapter 4.

Prayer is an interesting communication that we have the ability to do, but are often confused as to how or if we should do it. I am in no way an expert at prayer. As a matter of fact, I am still learning about prayer and how to approach it. However, what I do know is that I hear more people say that God doesn't answer or hear their prayers, rather than them admitting that there is something off on their end. Am I saying that God will only do for you based on you asking Him? No I'm not. What I am saying is just like any recipe, it must be done a certain way in order for you to get the desired results. One thing we should consider in prayer is that maybe this wasn't God's intention for how we would communicate with Him to begin with. I'm sure Adam and Eve had the freedom to speak to God. So how did we get to this place of having to even figure out how to pray?

Genesis 3:8 says, ***"And they heard the voice of the Lord God walking in the garden in the cool of the day: and Adam and his wife hid themselves from the presence of the Lord God amongst the trees of the garden. And the***

Lord God called unto Adam, and said unto him, Where art thou? And he said, I heard Thy voice in the garden, and I was afraid, because I was naked; and I hid myself." Some have said that the first time we see prayer is in Genesis 4:26. This was after Adam and Eve forfeited their relationship with God by listening to the serpent. Since they knew good and bad, right and wrong, this meant they had something to actually ask God to do to make something better for them. Therefore, after the birth of Seth, it says in Genesis 4:26, ***"And to Seth, to him also there was born a son; and he called his name Enos: then began men to call upon the name of the Lord."*** If this is truly the origin of prayer, I believe that man needed to pray, because the fall of man changed the way they communicated with God. As a result, they had to ask for what they wanted and what His will was in different situations.

We see now that if God gave prayer as a form of communication with Him and mankind, there is nothing wrong with it. What I mean is, whenever you see something going wrong with prayer, we must look at the breakdown in communication on man's end. After the fall, when Adam and Eve realized they did something wrong and heard God, they hid from Him, like so many of us do. Instead of going to God and talking out our issues, we make every effort to hide from Him. God obviously wanted to communicate with man, but when man messed up, he shut God out. We like to believe that this is on God, but that isn't true. Like so many of us, Adam and Eve made it seem like God didn't want to see them, but it was their idea to hide from God. This is one of the first issues in prayer, a breakdown in communication. When we fall short of the glory of God, the last thing we need to do is go away from Him. Distance from God is obviously how we get in the messes we get in.

I'm so grateful that God doesn't want us to do that. As a matter of fact, Hebrews 4:16 says, ***"Let us therefore come boldly to the throne of grace, that we may obtain mercy and find grace to help in time of need."*** If it feels like we are distant from God, it's because we didn't draw near to Him. The first thing God did with Adam was communicate His will for him. He wanted to let Adam know what to do to keep the life and lifestyle He intended for mankind. This lets us know He wants to communicate with us, to keep us in the loop as to what He wants for our life. God also shows us that He still wants us to come to Him when we fall short of His glory. Why? Because He is the only One Who can give us the grace we need to get and stay on the right track! We can't let sin or falling short of the glory of God stop us from communicating with Him, because He still wants us to talk/pray to Him. Notice that after the fall, Genesis 3:9 says God went looking for Adam and Eve. To me, this communicates that God wanted to talk to them! Would God go to them if He didn't want to talk? David didn't run from God when he sinned with Bathsheba. Psalm 51:1 says, ***"Have mercy upon me, O God, according to thy lovingkindness: according unto the multitude of thy tender mercies blot out my transgressions."***

When we sin, the response should be to go to God and not away from Him so that He can cleanse us from our sins.

Verses 2-4 says, ***"Wash me throughly from mine iniquity, and cleanse me from my sin. For I acknowledge my transgressions: and my sin is ever before me. Against thee, thee only, have I sinned, and done this evil in thy sight: that thou mightest be justified when thou speakest, and be clear when thou judgest."*** This is why David had such a good relationship with God. He didn't allow what he did wrong to wedge distance between him and God. It actually drew him closer to Him. He also acknowledged that he sinned against God and that he needed God to give him a fresh start. We have to understand that this was the entire purpose of Jesus dying on the Cross for us. He did it so that we could be reconciled back to God. Why? Because He wants us to have the access to talk to Him.

God no longer wanted someone talking on our behalf to Him. Christ's death removed the veil, giving us full access to God. 1 Peter 3:1 says, ***"For Christ also suffered once for sins, the righteous for the unrighteous, that He might bring us to God, being put to death in the flesh but made alive in the spirit,".*** This gives us the opportunity to go boldly to the Throne of Grace to obtain mercy (Hebrews 4:16). In prayer, we shouldn't make excuses, but admit our faults, acknowledge that we need Him, and accept the forgiveness and love He gives us!

HIS WILL:

Most people feel like God doesn't answer them even when they try to communicate, but remember, communication is a two way street. When we communicate with God, we aren't just telling Him our shortcomings. He also shares His will for our life. When we know His will, we can be assured that if our prayers align with that, we will most certainly have them. 1 John 5:14 says, ***"And this is the confidence that we have before Him: If we ask anything according to His will, He hears us."*** Our prayers may seem like they go unanswered, but really what it is, is that God won't allow us to be spoiled and have our way (will) over His Way (Will). If what we are asking for is not according to His will, He can either allow it or not, but your prayers aren't going unanswered. As a matter of fact, God isn't ignoring you because He is either saying one of these three things, yes, no, or not yet. We don't get the results we desire because we mess up this simple step in the recipe of "asking according to His will". James 4:3 says, ***"Ye ask, and receive not, because ye ask amiss, that ye may consume it upon your lusts."***

Our prayers aren't always necessities, let alone the will of God. Some of our prayers are selfish and meant to satisfy our flesh in some shape, form, or fashion. When we pray, we shouldn't communicate to God that we need or want something that is going to contradict His will for our lives because you can almost guarantee that you won't get the desired results. Even if He "allowed" it, you will end up all but begging Him to give you what His will was for you initially. Why? Because you will find out what His will was trying to protect you from. Another thing to realize is that God's will for our life is that His blessings, forgiveness, favor, etc. that He gives us, will be perpetuated in the earth. If what we ask Him for stops with us, it's not His will. Ask yourself, how can what I am asking God for be a blessing to someone else. This may help put you on the right track to getting the desired results because you're asking according to His will. It's not just for your life, but for those who will be impacted by what He gives/blesses you with.

Have Faith:

One of the other recipes in prayer is having faith. As a teacher, when I ask my students a question and their answer is in the form of a question, I know they're not confident their answer is correct. So many people ask God for something, but they're not confident they will receive it. This is one of the biggest no no's in the recipe to getting the desired results. James 1:6-8, ***"But let him ask in faith, nothing wavering. For he that wavereth is like a wave of the sea driven with the wind and tossed. For let not that man think that he shall receive any thing of the Lord. A double minded man is unstable in all his ways."*** You shouldn't think you're going to get it because you're not even sure He will or that He can give you what you're asking for. Peter was amazed that the fig tree Jesus cursed, actually withered when they came back to it.

Peter thought he would bring it to Jesus' attention as if Jesus was going to be just as shocked. However, Jesus was about to hip the disciples to the recipe of faith. Mark 11:22-24 says, ***"And Jesus answering saith unto them, Have faith in God. For verily I say unto you, That whosoever shall say unto this mountain, Be thou removed, and be thou cast into the sea; and shall not doubt in his heart, but shall believe that those things***

which he saith shall come to pass; he shall have whatsoever he saith. Therefore I say unto you, What things soever ye desire, when ye pray, believe that ye receive them, and ye shall have them." The idea isn't to have faith in yourself, but to have faith in God. Therefore when you pray, the mindset is that even before you ask, you know God can do it.

Forgiveness:

I can't conclude this section without calling out another mishap in the recipe for "getting your prayers answered". In the same moment of telling His disciples to have faith, He also revealed an important ingredient in prayer, which is forgiveness. He said in verses 25-26, ***"And when ye stand praying, forgive, if ye have ought against any: that your Father also which is in heaven may forgive you your trespasses. But if ye do not forgive, neither will your Father which is in heaven forgive your trespasses."*** You can tell Jesus was very serious about forgiveness in prayer because He also mentions it in the Lord's Prayer in Matthew 6:12, ***"And forgive us our debts, as we forgive our debtors."*** He was so serious about it that He doesn't even want us to bring Him any gift without forgiving others or making sure you haven't offended anyone without making it right.

Matthew 5:22-24 says, ***"But I say unto you, That whosoever is angry with his brother without a cause shall be in danger of the judgment: and whosoever shall say to his brother, Raca, shall be in danger of the council: but whosoever shall say, Thou fool, shall be in danger of hell***

fire. Therefore if thou bring thy gift to the altar, and there rememberest that thy brother hath ought against thee; Leave there thy gift before the altar, and go thy way; first be reconciled to thy brother, and then come and offer thy gift." So what does this have to do with prayer? The reason Jesus came was so our sins would be forgiven. Why? Because our sins kept us from God. So if you don't forgive, God won't forgive you. Matthew 6:14-15 says, ***"For if ye forgive men their trespasses, your heavenly Father will also forgive you: But if ye forgive not men their trespasses, neither will your Father forgive your trespasses."*** If you aren't forgiven by God, He won't be giving you anything else. What I mean by that is, when you don't forgive, you're holding on to something.

So how can God give you anything (forgiveness) and you are holding on to something already (unforgiveness). This means forgiveness is us letting what we have go, in order to receive what God has for us, which is forgiveness.

Trust:

I asked myself one day (November 15, 2022) a few questions that I feel like the Holy Spirit gave me the answers to. *Why do we pray?* For lack of something. *Why do we get hindered in prayer?* For the lack of something (ex. forgiveness). *Why do our prayers get answered?* To end lack. Remember when I said that prayer is a form of communication that was never a part of God's plan. The communication we had was cut off because Eve did not trust God's Word. This is one of the reasons why I feel we don't have our prayers "answered" is because we don't trust God. Trust is another one of those things that I feel that we lack when it comes to God. I am curious, did God do something that caused us not to trust Him or could it be that we did not follow the recipe and put the blame on Him?

If I had to answer for myself, I would say the latter. For example, when Adam ate the fruit and God asked him why, Genesis 3:12 says, ***"And the man said, The woman whom thou gavest to be with me, she gave me of the tree, and I did eat."*** If I had to translate that, I would say he was basically saying, *"God if you didn't give me this woman, I wouldn't have eaten the fruit."* What was it that made them question God's Word? I believe the serpent's agenda was to get Eve to not trust God and depend on her own logic. Proverbs 3:5-8 says, ***"Trust in the Lord with all thine heart; and lean not unto thine own understanding. In all thy ways acknowledge Him, and He shall direct thy paths."*** We are told to trust in the Lord with all of our heart, so we won't have room to trust ourselves more than we trust Him.

The moment Eve began to try to make sense of the situation, her reasoning got in the way. Proverbs 3:7-8 says, ***"Be not wise in thine own eyes: fear the Lord, and depart from evil. It shall be health to thy navel, and marrow to thy bones."*** God gave them the recipe, but Eve became wise in her eyes and didn't depart from evil (the serpent). When she decided to include the fruit in God's recipe, their health was compromised from that point forward. The enemy loves for us to question every recipe God has given us to follow. He would even love to convince us to add our own flavor to it. If you ever decide that you will go rogue with the recipe, all I can admonish you to do is to take responsibility for the outcome and not blame God.

Eve's thought should've been, *"Why would God even be intimidated by anything He created to the point that He would not tell the truth?"* Not having trust in prayer or not trusting to pray to begin with is a deep rooted issue that needs to be addressed. Most of us don't trust God in prayer because of disappointment. I am in no way perfect at this, but I have to consider that if it didn't happen, it wasn't supposed to and if it did, it was supposed to. God, in His infinite wisdom knows what's best for us. Jeremiah 29:11 says, ***"For I know the thoughts that I think toward you, saith the LORD, thoughts of peace, and not of evil, to give you an expected end."*** We have to trust that God has better intentions for us.

The one thing we don't have to doubt God on, is our needs! Jesus was trying to build the trust of His disciples as it pertained to provision of their necessities. He says in Matthew 6:25, ***"Therefore I say unto you, Take no thought for your life, what ye shall eat, or what ye shall drink; nor yet for your body, what ye shall put on. Is not the life more than meat, and the body than raiment? Behold the fowls of the air: for they sow not, neither do they reap, nor gather into barns; yet your heavenly Father feedeth them. Are ye not much better than they?"*** Jesus was trying to explain that the things He created that He doesn't have a relationship with like us and don't ask

Him for anything have their necessities, so why would it be a hard thing for Him to do for us, whom He has a relationship with?

God has shown us that His recipes work, so if He tells us not to worry, we should trust that. If He tells us not to do something, we should trust that. Every time we don't trust, we don't ask. Every time we don't ask, we don't receive. Unfortunately, every time we don't receive, we lose trust. The hardest part about that for me is, we will lose trust for not receiving what we didn't ask for as if we asked and He just didn't give it to us. In my opinion, we lack trust for all the wrong reasons. Again, when people lack trust, it is because of disappointment. However, we aren't given God a chance, but instead use that as an excuse to further not trust Him. This causes us to do what Eve did, trust others or ourselves.

Going back to Proverbs 3:5, it says, ***"Trust in the Lord with all your heart, and do not lean on your own understanding."*** We trust in ourselves as if the God of the universe doesn't have enough understanding to direct us. This pulls us away from prayer. However, when you trust in Him, it brings you back to a place of petitioning Him because in your humility you know that there is no other help aside from Him.

Lack of Communication:

One of today's biggest issues is the lack of communication in a technologically communicative world. What do I mean? Some of the main ways we communicate is using technology like cell phones, emails, social media, etc. Although these are great advancements, it has lessened the verbal and personal experience of communication. Most people would rather text than to talk on the phone, let alone talk in person. I, for one, am one of those people. However, if we are passing on these nonverbal skills to our children, then they will only have those nonverbal skills in communication… even with God. Sometimes people can barely communicate with God because their communication skills are questionable to begin with.

In the beginning, we had an amazing experience with God where He talked audibly with man. Imagine that! Unfortunately that ended after the fall of man. God stopped communicating with the entire human race verbally (some He still communicated with verbally) and from that point it was scary rather than normal to hear God's voice. Exodus 20:18-19 says, ***"And all the people saw the thunderings, and the lightnings, and the noise of the trumpet, and the mountain smoking: and when the people saw it, they removed, and stood afar off. And they said unto Moses, Speak thou with us, and we will hear: but let not God speak with us, lest we die."***

The people could no longer handle God's voice directly, so He began to handle communication the same way we are seeing it today. He went from verbally talking to us, to communicating with us by text. No, He didn't text message us, but He used the text, such as the commandments, the Law, and the scripture, to communicate with us. 2 Timothy 3:15-17 says, ***"And that from a child thou hast known the***

holy scriptures, which are able to make thee wise unto salvation through faith which is in Christ Jesus. All scripture is given by inspiration of God, and is profitable for doctrine, for reproof, for correction, for instruction in righteousness: That the man of God may be perfect, thoroughly furnished unto all good works." Even with the inspired text, if we don't understand it, it's almost like God didn't really speak to us.

The scripture is given by inspiration and don't get me wrong, the scripture is absolutely amazing for us to understand the mind of God, just like texting is an awesome substitute for communicating with someone. But that's all the text is, a substitute. The issue with text is that it's too many ways for people to misinterpret what you mean and in order to really know, you have to really know the person. When that person reveals to you the intent of their message, you understand it better. Which is why in order for us to fully understand the mind of God as it pertains to His text (scripture), we need God to reveal to us what that text means. Proverbs 25:2 says, ***"It is the glory of God to conceal a thing: but the honour of kings is to search out a matter."***

Fortunately, He still allows us to have communication with Him, but it takes effort on all our parts. When I say effort, I don't mean works, but I mean to communicate with anyone, you have to say and sometimes do something to make that happen. Therefore, it takes a little bit more to communicate with God. Deuteronomy 4:29 says, ***"But if from thence thou shalt seek the Lord thy God, thou shalt***

find him, if thou seek him with all thy heart and with all thy soul." Before I can really get into this scripture, I want to make sure that we better understand the word seek so that we can better understand what this verse is advising us to do.

I looked in the Strongs concordance and it says the word for seek in Hebrew is bâqash (pronounced baw-kash) It means, *"to search out (by any method, specifically in worship or prayer)".* This is what I meant by communication with God takes effort because if I am seeking after God, I can't just seek Him with just a little of me and accomplish much in prayer. Jeremiah 29:13 tells us, ***"And ye shall seek me, and find me, when ye shall search for me with all your heart."*** If I am seeking Him with all my heart, I go further than the surface. Seeking is me not just wanting to know His Name, but wanting to know Him. Therefore, the more I seek Him, the more I get to know about Him and His thoughts/plans for me.

The best communication God gives us is when we speak to Him ourselves and He speaks back. The Israelites were so uncomfortable with talking to God directly, they only wanted Moses to speak to Him on their behalf or just by the reading of the text. That's what has created this new norm of needing other people to speak to God on our behalf or only thinking that God speaks to certain people and not us. This is not to say that we don't need corporate prayer, but I also need to know how to go to God for myself so I can know Him personally. This is why God revealed so much to Moses because he spoke to Him beyond text. Exodus

33:11, ***"And the LORD spake unto Moses face to face, as a man speaketh unto his friend. And he turned again into the camp: but his servant Joshua, the son of Nun, a young man, departed not out of the tabernacle."***

The Israelites would've never needed Moses if God spoke to them face to face the same way He did Moses. Just like with technology, God's communication was not limited to just talking. He communicated with man in many different ways and through many different people. Job 33:14-17, ***"For God speaketh once, yea twice, yet man perceiveth it not. In a dream, in a vision of the night, when deep sleep falleth upon men, in slumberings upon the bed; Then he openeth the ears of men, and sealeth their instruction, That he may withdraw man from his purpose, and hide pride from man."*** If I call someone and I can't get in touch with them, I can text them the same message I am trying to tell them verbally. I can also facetime them or even try messaging them on social media. God is always trying to talk to us, but we don't always perceive it. So He uses other methods to communicate with us what we may have missed Him trying to say to us verbally.

You can find in scripture when God communicated with people in visions and in dreams. God spoke to Joseph twice in a dream. Once to tell him to take Mary as his wife (Matthew 1:20) and the other time to take Mary and Jesus and escape to Egypt (Matthew 2:13). He also came to Solomon in a dream to grant him whatever he asked for (1 Kings 3:5). God was not limited in his forms of communication. He even had a donkey to warn Balaam not to curse his people (Number 22:28-31). The point is we need to be very confident that God wants to talk to us and we need to put forth the same effort to communicate with Him as He does with us. If we don't we will continue to be ignorant of His plans and purpose for our lives. Why? We won't know what God's mind is if we don't communicate with Him to find out.

Jeremiah 29:11-12 says, ***"For I know the thoughts that I think toward you, saith the Lord, thoughts of peace, and not of evil, to give you an expected end. Then shall ye call upon me, and ye shall go and pray unto me, and I will hearken unto you."*** What a lot of people don't know is the back story behind this popular verse. God said this to Israel that after telling them that after their seventy years in captivity was accomplished, he would come back to them. The reason I am telling you this, is because that means that those remaining Israelites would not know the depths of God. The elders who knew God deeply would've died off by then and being in a foreign land, those remaining would lose that intimacy with God. So He wanted to make sure that the revenant would know that although they sinned against God and went into captivity for it, He was still going to be there to show them His love.

So God wanted to reestablish that, but He let them know that they would find Him if they put forth the effort to do it. Any relationship that you have, effort and time goes into that in order for it to be successful. This is because the more effort you put in it, the more time that it takes. Psalms 63:1, ***"O God, thou art my God; early will I seek Thee: my***

soul thirsteth for Thee, my flesh longeth for Thee in a dry and thirsty land, where no water is;". We see effort and time in play here because seeking takes time and he has to put in the effort to seek God early in the morning. The success of relationships is based on how well you all know each other because intent is revealed. We accomplish this in prayer. How? Communication is a two-way street. God doesn't want us, nor ask us to do all the talking in prayer. God wants to speak to us in prayer, just as much as He likes us to speak to Him.

If you were on a date, would you want to be the only one sharing how you feel about them or things they didn't know about you? Wouldn't you want them to do the same. That's why it's important for us to know that in prayer, it is not just a way for us to communicate with God, but for Him to also communicate with us. We tell Him things we think He doesn't know about us and as I said before He reveals things that we didn't know about Him or ourselves. Jeremiah 33:3 says, ***"Call unto me, and I will answer thee, and show thee great and mighty things, which thou knowest not."*** You see the exchange in that if we call (pray) to Him, He is telling us that he will answer us. When we do this it helps develop our relationship with Him more and more.

Relationship:

Before your relationship with God developed to a place of prayer, it may have been that you didn't go to Him in prayer at all. However, when we elevate to the place of prayer, we begin to get to know that if we call on Him, He hears us. Knowing Him also develops our confidence in Him. Paul encourages us in Philippians 4:6, which says, ***"Be careful for nothing; but in every thing by prayer and supplication with thanksgiving let your requests be made known unto God."*** For me this means, don't worry about nothing, but pray about everything. To go further, this means talking to God about everything (and anything). Imagine if we went to God about everything that we had a request for.

Most times we ask other people for what we need or we put in more hours at work, but we rarely ask God about it, let alone ask Him what we should do or if we should be doing it (whatever your "it" is) to begin with. If we decide to pray less, we're choosing to worry more. That's not to say that God is saying in order to pray more, you need to be wordy in prayer. As a matter of fact, Jesus said in Matthew 6:7, ***"But when ye pray, use not vain repetitions, as the heathen do: for they think that they shall be heard for their much speaking."*** What Jesus is simply saying is He wants you to talk to Him and although it doesn't say it specifically in this verse, He wants us to talk to Him often. 1 Thessalonians 5:17 says, ***"Pray without ceasing."*** Why? Because His original purpose was to have a relationship with us and that relationship involves communication and prayer is that communication.

God is after the development of that relationship. He wants us to advance in that relationship from God and man to Father and child. That relationship can never develop without communication. The more I communicate with someone, the more I learn about the nature of that person. I can answer questions honestly like, *"Is this person dependable?"* Or *"Does this person really love me?"* This builds your confidence in a person that they are who they say that they are. In the case with our relationship with God, that confidence is called faith. Galatians 3:26 says, ***"For ye are all the children of God by faith in Christ Jesus."*** Once we get to the place of faith, we get to experience that relationship with God that He intended to re-establish through Christ. That relationship is that between Father and child.

God didn't need us as sons, He wanted us as sons. There is a big difference! If God already had a Son, whom He loved very much, why would He ever want us? Simple, He has always loved us. It didn't just start! Jeremiah 31:3 says, ***"The LORD hath appeared of old unto me, saying, Yea, I have loved thee with an everlasting love: therefore with lovingkindness have I drawn thee."*** I can make pretty much any R&B song a worship song I sing to the Lord or one that I feel like He's singing to me. There is this one Barry White song that says, *"I've got so much to give, to you my dear. It's going to take a lifetime. It's going to take years."* I love that song, but Barry White said it will take a lifetime to give her all of his love. As good as that sounds, my boy Barry falls short of how long God has, is, and will love us! Do you know how long everlasting is?! Merriam-Webster calls it for all time or in the words of Bible Study Tools, it has no beginning or end. I didn't always understand this word until my assistant pastor, Elder Don Thompson said it to me in conversation. I think he assumed I knew because of how casually he said it in conversation. Honestly, I think I understood the forever part of it, but I didn't understand the always existing, past tense part of it.

The new revelation I had of the word everlasting wowed me! Think about it! The Father's everlasting love means He always has, He always is, and always will love us! That's love! And that love is the love that motivated God and His Son to give so much so that we can be back in relationship with Him. 1 John 3:1 says, ***"Behold, what manner of love the Father hath bestowed upon us, that we should be called the sons of God: therefore the world knoweth us not, because it knew Him not."*** God wanted to re-established that relationship between God and man through His Son Jesus, our sin wouldn't allow for us to be in relationship with Him. That means we couldn't communicate with Him for ourselves to establish a relationship of our own. God didn't want this to continue to be His relationship with man. Therefore, Jesus had to come fix that, in order to bring us back into fellowship with God. This is why we can't get to God except we go through Jesus first. If Jesus is the reason our relationship with God was re-established, that means He holds weight in our communication (prayer life) with God.

IN THE NAME OF JESUS:

The recipe for prayer calls for us to pray in the Name of Jesus, but we can't do that just based on our relationship with God. The truth is we can't have this relationship with God or access to this relationship with God without a relationship with Christ. That's because we can't get to God without Jesus and more importantly, we can't talk to God without the NAME OF JESUS. Jesus explained in John 16:24, ***"Hitherto have ye asked nothing in My name: ask, and ye shall receive, that your joy may be full."*** Our prayers and petitions should be made in Jesus' Name because He promises to get involved. He promises that if we ask in His Name, God will do it. 1 John 2:1 says, ***"My little children, these things write I unto you, that ye sin not. And if any man sin, we have an advocate with the Father, Jesus Christ the Righteous:"*** God will do it because Jesus will advocate for us.

I can remember I asked my mom if I could get my bellybutton pierced and she said no. When I told my sister that my mom said no, she said she was going to ask her for me. Jesus does the same thing for us when we pray to the Father. Jesus told His disciples in John 16:26, ***"At that day ye shall ask in My name: and I say not unto you, that I will pray the Father for you:".*** Maybe you're like me thinking what difference would it make if my sister asked my mom for me. What was the big difference between me asking my mom and my sister asking my mom? Well, I believe that my sister said one key thing that really made my mom say yes. After my sister asked my mom if I could get it, she sealed it with, *"And I will pay for it."* Jesus is being the Big Brother, advocating on our behalf to the Father and the reason the Father says yes, is because Jesus reminds Him that He already paid for our sins.

When that sacrifice is so moving to God, He will do it because Jesus His Son asked on our behalf. I am that way with my own kids. When one of their siblings asks for something on the other's behalf, I just get moved to say yes. Why? It's because I love that they love each other enough that they will use whatever favor they feel like they have with me to ask for each other. I especially love that it is not for their personal gain, but just because they love each other. This is how the Father responds to when we ask things in Jesus Name, John 16:27 says, ***"For the Father himself loveth you, because ye have loved me, and have believed that I came out from God."*** The recipe is not to ask for it in your own name, but in your Big Brother Jesus Name because He knows what to say to get the Father to say yes to you.

1 Thessalonians 5:17 says, ***"Pray without ceasing."***

YOU'RE THE PROBLEM, NOT... AUTHORITY Chapter 5.

You may be one of those people who hates authority, but hopefully after this, you will feel differently. Romans 13:1 says, ***"Let every soul be subject unto the higher powers. For there is no power but of God: the powers that be are ordained of God."*** In some translations it says be subject to governing authorities. Anyone who has been given authority over you, whether government, boss, husband, parents, etc., we are to be subject to them. Now, I don't want to lose an audience here, so just hold tight and I will do my best to break all of this down. Let's first consider that we have to have leadership. I understand that not all leadership is good because Proverbs 29:2 says, ***"When the righteous are in authority, the people rejoice: but when the wicked beareth rule, the people mourn."*** I think one of the biggest problems that people have with authority is that they've had a bad experience with them. However, we can't let bad experiences cause us to rebel against what God's Word (the recipe) is telling us to do.

Going back to Romans 13:1, the word subject can seem so demeaning that you would want to completely disregard it!

If you define the word subject, it means to place under, subject to, or obey. Before we go in depth with this definition, I will first like to begin with the word under. On your job, you rank under your boss, correct? Therefore, you are taking commands from him or her. This doesn't make you less than them as a person, but it makes you under their direction or lead. This does not happen because you are insignificant in any way. Instead, it happens because they have (or should have) more knowledge or experience to lead you. If you follow their lead, one day you may acquire the same, if not more knowledge and experience. Galatians 4:1-5 says, ***"Now I say, That the heir, as long as he is a child, differeth nothing from a servant, though he be lord of all; But is under tutors and governors until the time appointed of the father. Even so we, when we were children, were in bondage under the elements of the world: But when the fulness of the time was come, God sent forth His Son, made of a woman, made under the law, To redeem them that were under the law, that we might receive the adoption of sons."***

That passage says a lot, but let's break it down. The types of leadership over us can be parents, teachers/tutors, government officials, etc. We should look at authority, not as a reason to rebel, but a way of governing us until the appointed time for us to exercise our leadership or grow to a place where God has called us to be. That was the purpose of the law. It governed us. When I say governed us, it not only directed us, but gave us the pattern for Godly living. Although we are no longer under the Law of the Old Testament, there are still laws and rules that we must submit to, as well as leadership. We won't be perfect under leadership, however, we shouldn't rebel against it because we will lose out on the opportunity to learn what we need to when it's our turn to lead. Our mindset should be, even Jesus was under the authority of His earthly father Joseph until an appointed time. This should help us change our mindset and realize that by following well, we become better leaders.

Unfortunately, a lot of people don't see it that way. They regulate on their boss or even disregard what they've been asked to do. However, they're not going to create a solution like that. The more you resist or usurp authority, the more problems you will have. One of the reasons you may have problems could be a number of things, but one is found in Job 4:8, which says, ***"As I have observed, those who plow iniquity and those who sow trouble reap the same."*** If you ever have a desire to lead or are ever put in a position of authority and you've only rebelled against authority, you would be arrogant to think that your disregard for authority will not show up later in your life in some form. God has a way of showing you yourself in order to help you learn from it. If you ignore it, you can be vexed as a result of it. You are setting yourself up to reap a harvest of rebellion in your seasons of leadership.

Galatians 6:7 says, ***"Be not deceived; God is not mocked: for whatsoever a man soweth, that shall he also reap."*** When this happens most people are shocked and wonder why it's happening to them. They begin to blame the person or everything else, rather than admit to themselves that they are reaping a harvest of the bad seeds they've sown. The fact is that it's them that needs the work. Let's make it more relatable. What if your children ignore everything you say and you can't seem to understand why. God isn't pleased with your children's rebellion! However, earlier that day your boss asked you to do something and you blatantly ignored him/her. God isn't pleased with that either! What you may be seeing at home is what your boss sees at work, rebellion. God set you as an authority in your home for your children because they need guidance. No, you're not an expert just because God gave you children, but Romans 8:30 says, ***"Moreover whom He did predestinate, them He also called: and whom He called, them He also justified: and whom He justified, them He also glorified."***

In this case, God determined ahead of time (predestination) that He would call (called) you righteous (justified) for a position you weren't qualified for, yet He will give you what you need to be and look amazing (glorified) at it. However, if we don't recognize this in those that are in an authoritative position in our lives, how can we expect that anyone would see this in our own lives? We rejoice about Romans 8:30, but we are quick to judge those ranked higher than us and call them unqualified. Take a moment and ask yourself, *"What do my critics say about me in the position of authority I'm in?"* All of us at some point, in some way have had some type of position of authority and whether we felt qualified or not, the truth is, none of us are. None of us should be ranked over anyone because we are human and subject to error. One error in someone's eyes, makes us unqualified in their opinion. This is why it says in Romans 12:3, ***"For I say, through the grace given unto me, to every man that is among you, not to think of himself more highly than he ought to think; but to think soberly, according as God hath dealt to every man the measure of faith."*** I'm saying this because I'm wondering how you would like to be treated?

Now I have to be gentle with this topic because I'm not saying God has placed everyone that's over you in that position. There are some jerks and unqualified people in a lot of positions of authority that God isn't cosigning on. However, that doesn't give us a right to usurp authority. Scripture tells us what to do with those that are in authority. 1 Timothy 2:1-4 says, ***"I exhort therefore, that, first of all, supplications, prayers, intercessions, and giving of thanks, be made for all men; For kings, and for all that are in authority; that we may lead a quiet and peaceable life in all godliness and honesty. For this is good and acceptable in the sight of God our Saviour; Who will have all men to be saved, and to come unto the knowledge of the truth."*** Even with the most foolish leader, God has never given us permission to bash them or be disrespectful. He encourages us to pray for them because what we pray about can change the course of things. Either God will change them or remove them!

Disclaimer: If there is any threat of danger or illegal activity, I am not telling you to stick around! Alert the authorities and make the decision that God is leading

you to make for you and your family's safety and freedom!

It is understood that bad leadership is a difficult thing to handle. Again, Proverbs 29:2 says, ***"When the righteous are in authority, the people rejoice: But when the wicked beareth rule, the people mourn."*** This is why it is so important for you to know how to follow and serve well. God is raising up a new set of leaders who will rule and lead in righteousness, but if we respond to their bad leadership with rebellion, we may repeat the cycle. In 1 Kings 12, Jeroboam tried to get king Rehoboam (king Solomon's son) to make a decision to treat his people better than his father did. When Rehoboam took the horrible advice of his friends (1 Kings 12:10-14), the nation was split, one part rebelling with Jeroboam and making him their king. However, he didn't turn out to be the best leader either. This may have appeared like the right thing to do, but what's interesting is that king Jeroboam was paranoid that the people would eventually rebel against him and go back to king Rehoboam.

1 Kings 12:26-30 - says, ***"And Jeroboam said in his heart, Now shall the kingdom return to the house of David: If this people go up to do sacrifice in the house of the LORD at Jerusalem, then shall the heart of this people turn again unto their lord, even unto Rehoboam king of Judah, and they shall kill me, and go again to Rehoboam king of Judah. Whereupon the king took counsel, and made two calves of gold, and said unto them, It is too much for you to go up to Jerusalem: behold thy gods, O Israel, which brought thee up out of the land of Egypt***

And he set the one in Bethel, and the other put he in Dan. And this thing became a sin: for the people went to worship before the one, even unto Dan." Of course this was bound to happen because this was prophesied to happen due to Solomon's sin (1 Kings 11:11-13). However, his response had him paranoid, causing him to make Israel to sin by worshiping idol gods!

When you remain consistent in doing well, no one around you can say anything. Even if they tried to say something bad initially, your consistent good behavior silences the hate. 1 Peter 2:13-16 says, ***"Submit yourselves to every ordinance of man for the Lord's sake: whether it be to the king, as supreme; Or unto governors, as unto them that are sent by him for the punishment of evildoers, and for the praise of them that do well. For so is the will of God, that with well doing ye may put to silence the ignorance of foolish men: As free, and not using your liberty for a cloke of maliciousness, but as the servants of God."*** Saul wasn't the best king, but David served him well. Unfortunately, Saul became jealous of David. He spoke harshly against him and even tried to kill him, but David honored God, by honoring king Saul.

By David not trying to seek revenge on king Saul, it only rebuked him and made him apologize for treating him that way. 1 Samuel 26:21 says, ***"Then said Saul, I have sinned: return, my son David: for I will no more do thee harm, because my soul was precious in thine eyes this day: behold, I have played the fool, and have erred exceedingly."*** For most of us, if this happened, we would have tried to respond maliciously. However, God wants us to let Him get revenge for us, especially as it pertains to those in leadership. It's not our place to correct them, but God's. 1 Timothy 5:1 says, ***"Rebuke not an elder, but intreat him as a father; and the younger men as brethren;".*** David had an opportunity to take revenge on king Saul, but even when he was encouraged to do it, it said in 1 Samuel 26:8-11, ***"Then said Abishai to David, God hath delivered thine enemy into thine hand this day: now therefore let me smite him, I pray thee, with the spear even to the earth at once, and I will not smite him the second time. And David said to Abishai, Destroy him not: for who can stretch forth his hand against the LORD'S anointed, and be guiltless? David said furthermore, As the LORD liveth, the LORD shall smite him; or his day shall come to die; or he shall descend into battle, and perish. The LORD forbid that I should stretch forth mine hand against the LORD'S anointed: but, I pray thee, take thou now the spear that is at his bolster, and the cruse of water, and let us go."***

Had David taken that opportunity to kill king Saul, he wouldn't have seen the Hand of the Lord deliver him. He also would've created more drama for himself because as David said, killing God's anointed would've made him guilty. Just because it seemed like the right response, killing Saul would've done nothing but probably made David paranoid. When someone tried to make themselves look good in David's eyes by saying they killed Saul, they didn't get the reward they were looking for. 2 Samuel 1:14-16 says, ***"And David said unto him, How wast thou***

not afraid to stretch forth thine hand to destroy the LORD'S anointed? And David called one of the young men, and said, Go near, and fall upon him. And he smote him that he died. And David said unto him, Thy blood be upon thy head; for thy mouth hath testified against thee, saying, I have slain the LORD'S anointed." We shouldn't try seeking revenge on our leadership or those in authority, especially God's anointed, because we forfeit what God has planned for us.

Again, this is not to say that God is for wicked rulers/leadership. This is also not me saying that you should tolerate someone who is threatening your life or doing illegal things. I believe in those cases, pray and ask God for wisdom to get out of those situations! The only thing I am trying to do is admonish you in the Word, to allow God to fight your battles and in the meantime, be light in darkness. When being light, God doesn't want you to compromise your integrity, but He does want us to pray for them, because they are obviously misguided. God wants us to pray for His influence in the lives of the people that are in the position of leadership in the earth realm. Leadership is not always an employer and employee relationship. It can also be a parent(s) and child(ren) relationship as well. However, when it comes to these relationships, we use a different word with our parents that we don't always use with authority and that is obey.

Colossians 3:20 says, ***"Children, obey your parents in all things: for this is well pleasing unto the Lord."*** The Strong's and King James definition of the word obey means, *"to hear under (as a subordinate), listen attentively, to heed or conform to a command or authority."* Why should we obey our parents? Is it because God wants us to make them feel good or even make them feel superior? No. It's not to please anyone, but God. How does it please God? If God puts anyone in charge, they represent His authority. So we respect and obey our parent because they are an extension of God's authority in our life. Not only that, but He's teaching us at a young age how to respond to Him as our Father. We have to ask ourselves, *"Would we handle God the same way we handle our parents?"* Better question, *"Would it be appropriate to handle God the way you handle your parents?"* If not, we should reevaluate our obedience to our parents' authority.

For most of us, as little children, we obeyed our parents. Somewhere in the teenage years, this took a turn and we threw "listening to your parents" out the window. However, at the beginning of our lives, God gives different authority in the earth to lead us and those are our parents. Hebrews 13:17 says, ***"Obey them that have the rule over you, and submit yourselves: for they watch for your souls, as they that must give account, that they may do it with joy, and not with grief: for that is unprofitable for you."*** This applies to anyone who has rule over you, but this definitely applies to your parents. God's Word tells us to do this, because there is a great responsibility parents have on rearing kids and helping them to be the best version of themselves that He created them to be. They actually have to give an account to God for being parents! We think that we can just turn on and off obedience with certain people, but it's not that easy. Do you think that if you can't obey your parents, you will obey God? Look at 1 John 4:20, which says, ***"If a man say, I love God, and hateth his brother, he is a liar: for he that loveth not his brother whom he hath seen, how can he love God whom he hath not seen?".*** Although this talks about a brother, whether siblings (brother or sister) or those in Christ (brother or sister), I feel like it applies to pretty much every relational situation.

If we are honest, we will not obey God, Whom we don't physically see, if we don't obey our parents, whom we do see. God teaches us how to handle His authority over our lives, beginning with the first one we encounter, our parents. If we handle this correctly, when we get older and get a job, we can handle authority in the workplace. From there, we can grow in our personal relationship with God and revere His authority. This is why you can tell which adults were rebellious as a child because they are usually the ones who are rebellious at their jobs or to other authority in different aspects of their adult lives. They are usually (not all the time, but usually) the ones with little to no respect to those in authority because if they do it at an early age, they develop a mindset that there is no need for authority over them.

Whether people acknowledge it or not, obedience is very vital to our development, especially as future leaders (parents, CEO's, etc.). It is also crucial to our production. What do I mean? If an adult was once a disobedient child that grew up to be an rebellious adult, when they have children, what type of children do you think they will produce? Nowhere does it say that the priest Eli was a rebellious child, however, he had to have had some type of disobedience or lack of discipline. When it describes Eli, it says that he was overweight (1 Samuel 4:18). I'm not saying that him being overweight means he was disobedient, but it was noted for a reason and I believe it was because as a priest, he should've had restraint/discipline. So, his disobedience may not have been to his earthly parents, but if God was telling him to have restraint and he didn't, that's still disobedience. This turned out to be the problem that his sons had as well.

1 Samuel 2:22-25 , ***"Now Eli was very old, and heard all that his sons did unto all Israel; and how they lay with the women that assembled at the door of the tabernacle of the congregation. And he said unto them, Why do ye such things? for I hear of your evil dealings by all this people. Nay, my sons; for it is no good report that I hear: ye make the Lord's people to transgress. If one man sin against another, the judge shall judge him: but if a man sin against the Lord, who shall intreat for him? Notwithstanding they hearkened not unto the voice of their father, because the Lord would slay them."*** Eli didn't obey his duty as priest, because he didn't hold his children accountable. The important takeaway from these rebellious children is that although they rebelled against their father, their greatest rebellion was against God! I say that because they were adults and a part of the priesthood. Therefore, there should not just be honor for your parents, but honor and a reverential fear of God even the more.

Ephesians 6:1-3 says, ***"Children, obey your parents in the Lord: for this is right. Honour thy father and mother; which is the first commandment with promise; That it may be well with thee, and thou mayest live long on the earth."*** Paul tells children to obey their parents, but in Exodus 20:12, it is a commandment to honor your father and mother. King James bible defines honor as, *"The esteem due or paid to worth; high estimation."* Their honor for their father, would have caused them to take heed to his words. These weren't about them rebelling against him as their father, but he was advising them in regards to their priestly office. This is why their sin wasn't against their father, but against God. Unfortunately, their apathy and rebellion against God would catch up with them. 1 Samuel 3:10-11 says, ***"And the Philistines fought, and Israel was smitten, and they fled every man into his tent: and there was a very great slaughter; for there fell of Israel thirty thousand footmen. And the ark of God was taken; and the two sons of Eli, Hophni and Phinehas, were slain."***

Not only were Eli's sons killed, but they were the reason the Ark of God was taken. You can't expect God's favor and you're rebellious against authority and/or your parents! It may not seem like a big deal, but it affects everything around you. We have to remember that obedience is not something that is difficult. It is only difficult in the absence of humility. Philippians 2:5-8 says, ***"Let this mind be in you, which was also in Christ Jesus: Who, being in the form of God, thought it not robbery to be equal with God: But made Himself of no reputation, and took upon Bim***

the form of a servant, and was made in the likeness of men: And being found in fashion as a man, He humbled Himself, and became obedient unto death, even the death of the cross." Jesus gave us the recipe on how to properly handle authority. He first had the mind to obey. His thoughts weren't high, but humble. He wasn't reminding God of Who He is, but He removed His reputation and obeyed.

If His mindset wasn't obedience, Jesus would've told God, *"Get somebody else to do it."* Jesus is One of the three Persons of the Holy Trinity. However, what made Him obey the Father was that He had a humble mindset. What I am trying to say is that we have no excuse! NONE! Matthew 11:29 AMPC says, ***"Take My yoke upon you and learn of Me, for I am gentle (meek) and humble (lowly) in heart, and you will find rest (relief and ease and refreshment and recreation and blessed quiet) for your souls."*** Jesus said that we should learn of or from Him these things, that He is gentle (meek) and humble (lowly) in heart. Therefore, if Jesus was humble enough to be obedient to His Father, children should and can be humble enough to be obedient to their parents. If Jesus was humble enough to obey God, employees should be humble enough to comply and adhere to their employer.

Rebellion was never the solution for the believer because the results are rejection. 1 Samuel 15:22-23 says, ***"And Samuel said, Hath the LORD as great delight in burnt offerings and sacrifices, as in obeying the voice of the LORD? Behold, to obey is better than sacrifice, and to***

hearken than the fat of rams. For rebellion is as the sin of witchcraft, and stubbornness is as iniquity and idolatry. Because thou hast rejected the word of the LORD, he hath also rejected thee from being king." I believe the consequences for disobedience are so harsh because our disobedience (sin) can be the influence of someone else's rebellion (sin). That was the problem after the fall of man. From one act of disobedience, came sin and that sin birth different types of sin like rebellion and and as vs. 23 says, that turns into witchcraft. So our obedience is key for great future leadership. 2 Timothy 2:1-2 says, ***"Thou therefore, my son, be strong in the grace that is in Christ Jesus. And the things that thou hast heard of me among many witnesses, the same commit thou to faithful men, who shall be able to teach others also."***

Also, Philippians 4:9 says, ***"Those things, which ye have both learned, and received, and heard, and seen in me, do: and the God of peace shall be with you."*** If it's good leadership and we follow it, we can teach others to do the same and that obedience makes for our peace! Luke 6:40 says, ***"The disciple is not above his master: but every one that is perfect shall be as his master."*** If the leadership you've submitted under is not good, remember 1 Timothy 2:1- says, ***"I exhort therefore, that, first of all, supplications, prayers, intercessions, and giving of thanks, be made for all men; For kings, and for all that are in authority; that we may lead a quiet and peaceable life in all godliness and honesty. For this is good and acceptable in the sight of God our Saviour; Who will have all men to be saved, and to come unto the knowledge of***

the truth." Don't talk about them, pray for them, so that God can bless and change them to lead better.

Just remember, no matter how old or what the position is, if we can all humble ourselves and submit to the authority that God has placed in our lives, we learn to lead better lives and others!

1 Peter 2:13 says, ***"Submit yourselves to every ordinance of man for the Lord's sake: whether it be to the king, as supreme;".***

YOU'RE THE PROBLEM, NOT...

PEACE Chapter 6.

The reason most of us don't have peace is because we don't understand it. Peace is defined as a state of tranquility or peace between individuals, meaning they are in a harmonious relationship. The word tranquil means, *"calm, serenity, calmness, placid, placidity, stillness"*. In order for us to gain this state of being, we have to be aware that it is a such thing and it is attainable in almost any situation. Why? Well one of the reasons for this chapter is that in most situations we are in, we don't realize the situation may not be the problem. Let me give this disclaimer, I am not saying that this is always the case. However, there is something that is more of a problem than anything else and that is our perspective.

Most times, we tell ourselves that if the situation changes, then we will have peace. Unfortunately, that is not always true. We don't realize that by saying that, we are admitting that if the situation doesn't change, we will always be in a place opposite of peace. If you are a believer, then you know that that is not true! Although the chapter is called,

"You're the Problem, Not Peace", I don't mean that you are the one causing the problem in the situation, whatever that situation may be. I mean that you're the problem if you think that the only way you can have peace is if the situation is perfect/erased. 2 Thessalonians 3:16 says, ***"Now may the Lord of peace Himself give you peace at all times and in every way. The Lord be with all of you."*** The Amplified Classic Translation says, ***"Now may the Lord of peace Himself grant you His peace (the peace of His Kingdom) at all times and in all ways [under all circumstances and conditions, whatever comes]. The Lord [be] with you all."***

I want to first discuss the fact that peace is not obtained by anything or anyone created in the earth. Peace comes from God and from God only. Romans 1:7 says, ***"To all that be in Rome, beloved of God, called to be saints: Grace to you and peace from God our Father, and the Lord Jesus Christ."*** God our Father and Jesus, our Lord, gives us peace. Galatians 5:22 also tells us that one of the fruits of the Spirit is peace. You see that the Triune God (Father, Son, Holy Spirit) gives of our peace! This means peace is a divine thing and since it's divine, we can't base it on things and people. Paul's prayer in 2 Thessalonians 3:16 didn't differentiate what times or situations a person has peace. Instead, he prayed that God would give them peace at all times and in every way.

I can remember thinking how I needed a situation to change in order for me to have peace. If I would've continued to think that way, I would still be in a place of conflict to this day! I didn't have peace because I couldn't control certain situations or people. When God revealed to me the things I needed to focus my attention on, which were the things I could control or change about myself, I no longer focused my attention on people or things I couldn't change. Why? Because that's why I couldn't be at peace. God showed me the things I needed to work on and towards, and when I only focused on that, there was a peace I received that I couldn't or shouldn't be able to understand.

Peace Misunderstood:

The reason the peace of God is not understood is because nothing changed around you or about the situation, except the way you view your situation. Let's look at one of the best examples of this found in 2 Kings 6:15-17 says, ***"And when the servant of the man of God was risen early, and gone forth, behold, an host compassed the city both with horses and chariots. And his servant said unto him, Alas, my master! how shall we do? And he answered, Fear not: for they that be with us are more than they that be with them. And Elisha prayed, and said, Lord, I pray thee, open his eyes, that he may see. And the Lord opened the eyes of the young man; and he saw: and, behold, the mountain was full of horses and chariots of fire round about Elisha."*** Elisha didn't pray that God would make the army disappear (change the situation). He prayed that his servant could have the eyes to see the situation better.

From the point that God opened his servant's eyes, they handled and saw the situation differently, even though the situation wasn't different. We have to stop praying for God to remove the situation, and begin praying that God will change how we see it, so that we can face it. The confidence that we have in any and all situations is that when God is in it with us, no matter how it looks, we win! Mark 4:37-39 says, ***"And there arose a great storm of wind, and the waves beat into the ship, so that it was now full. And He was in the hinder part of the ship, asleep on a pillow: and they awake Him, and say unto Him, Master, carest Thou not that we perish? And He arose, and rebuked the wind, and said unto the sea, Peace, be still. And the wind ceased, and there was a great calm."*** So many takeaways in this passage of scripture, but let's begin with Jesus' response to the storm.

We have all heard how Jesus slept during the storm and that is some peace that we should all admire, but what we really should look at is when He had peace and when the storm calmed. Jesus was asleep during the storm. I know that there are a lot of people who have said that they have slept through a storm, but this wasn't your ordinary "I slept through noise" kind of storm. Jesus slept through the wind and the waves beating up on the ship and water filling it. That wasn't Jesus just sleeping hard, but it was Him at peace. He knew that His assignment wasn't complete, so danger or death weren't a threat to Him. This had to have been the assurance He needed to remain asleep. While Jesus rested in His peace that God would keep them, the disciples stayed up worrying.

People may argue that Jesus slept because He is God in the flesh and the disciples are merely human. I get that and that is a great point, but the disciples were at an extreme advantage too! They were on the boat with Jesus! Can you imagine being on a boat with Jesus and worrying about if you would die? I am not surprised that Jesus' response to the disciples' panic in Mark 4:40, which says, ***"And He said unto them, Why are ye so fearful? how is it that ye have no faith?"*** Sometimes we worry that we aren't going to get to our destination because the journey isn't smooth. Psalms 55:22 says, ***"Cast thy burden upon the Lord, and He shall sustain thee: He shall never suffer the righteous to be moved."*** Jesus is teaching us in the verse that your journey can be turbulent, but that doesn't mean you should immediately think that you are doomed to fail.

I believe that God wouldn't call me to do anything that I will fail at, unless the failure is a part of His will for me to succeed. When we experience anything that doesn't feel quite harmonious, it isn't because God doesn't want us to have peace, but it gives value to the peace we have. Jesus sleeping through the storm wasn't just about peace, but He may have been tired. Think about it, Jesus prayed all night before choosing His disciples. He would spend the day teaching and/or healing. So, He genuinely probably needed the rest. Matthew 11:28-29 says, ***"Come unto Me, all ye that labour and are heavy laden,***

and I will give you rest. Take My yoke upon you, and learn of Me; for I am meek and lowly in heart: and ye shall find rest unto your souls."

That entire ship situation was a teachable moment for the disciples. Jesus wants us to have rest and in order to get it we must go to Him to get it. It wasn't that the disciples didn't come to Jesus because they did. However, the problem was when they came to Him they weren't coming to get rest, but to worry and panic. His disciples should've said to themselves, *"If this is His response to the storm, I will respond the same way."* Instead, the disciples allowed their fear to rob them of peace. The absence of peace means the absence of rest. If rest was important to Jesus, then He wants us to have rest too! If we don't come to Him and learn His ways, we won't be able to operate like Him and be at rest, no matter how much He wants this for us. Jesus didn't let the disturbance hinder the necessary rest He needed for the next journey.

His peace allowed Him to do what was healthy for Him. There is no way that you can be at peace and worry at the same time. We know that Jesus was at peace because sleep is an indicator that you are not worried. God preceded rest with something very important, peace. Being on the ship with Jesus should've been enough to give them peace to sleep on top of the water, yet they still doubted, like most of us do. Jesus' promises in scripture should hold the same, if not greater weight with us today. Why? Because we actually have the examples that the disciples didn't. The disciples were waiting for the storm to calm in order for them to feel at peace. However, Jesus had what Isaiah 26:3 calls perfect peace.

This peace allowed Him to sleep while in the midst of the storm. If we are absent of peace, I can almost guarantee that, like the disciples, you're deprived of sleep. This is because instead of the disciples resting in their peace, they probably stayed up worrying all night. Psalm 127:2 says, ***"It is vain for you to rise up early, to sit up late, to eat the bread of sorrows: For so He giveth His beloved sleep."*** God may call you to all night prayer, like Jesus did, but He will never call you to all night worrying. Quite honestly, it was a waste of the disciples time to worry when they had the Savior on board with them. The worst that could've happened was they would've gotten thrown in the sea and Jesus would've had to have saved them. Either way, they worried about something that they shouldn't have. We know that the lack of sleep is not a part of God's design because, as we read before, God gives those He loves sleep.

I am sure that this seems like I am making this easier said than done. However, there are examples of people being at peace in the midst of their own personal "storms". David was one of them. In Psalms, David realized how many people were up against him. Psalms 3:1-3 says, ***"Lord, how are they increased that trouble me! many are they that rise up against me. Many there be which say of my soul, There is no help for him in***

God. Selah. But thou, O LORD, art a Shield for me; my Glory, and the Lifter up of mine head." This had to have been terrifying because David's own son, Absalom, rebelled against him and got others to join his rebellion. David could've let this disturb his peace, and honestly he probably allowed it to for a moment, until he put his trust in God. Verses 4-6 says, ***"I cried unto the LORD with my voice, and He heard me out of His holy hill. Selah. I laid me down and slept; I awaked; for the LORD sustained me. I will not be afraid of ten thousands of people, that have set themselves against me round about."***

Although all of this was coming against him, David's peace allowed him to sleep. The situation didn't change around David, but his mindset about the situation did! Unfortunately, most people miss out on their experience with peace because they focus more on the situation changing rather than their mindset changing about the situation. Paul says something very helpful in Philippians 4:6-8, ***"Be careful for nothing; but in every thing by prayer and supplication with thanksgiving let your requests be made known unto God. And the peace of God, which passeth all understanding, shall keep your hearts and minds through Christ Jesus. Finally, brethren, whatsoever things are true, whatsoever things are honest, whatsoever things are just, whatsoever things are pure, whatsoever things are lovely, whatsoever things are of good report; if there be any virtue, and if there be any praise, think on these things."***

Anxiety is a sign of no peace, so Paul is saying don't worry about your situation, but give that concern to God by telling Him about it, and from there God will give you something in exchange, peace. How does this happen? If I replace the devil's lies with God's Truth, I don't have any worries, because God's Word will come to pass. Let's look at another example of how this worked for David. Psalms 46:1-3 says, ***"God is our Refuge and Strength, a very Present Help in trouble. Therefore will not we fear, though the earth be removed, and though the mountains be carried into the midst of the sea; Though the waters thereof roar and be troubled, though the mountains shake with the swelling thereof. Selah."*** The whole earth could be removed and yet, David kept his mind on what is true, ***"God is our Refuge and Strength, a very Present Help in trouble."*** Keeping his mind on God's promises gave him peace in the midst of what was going on.

I don't know if you can experience peace like that if you don't have your mind on God and His promises. This is why Paul advised the Philippians to watch how they thought about things, because he knew that the way we think about things contributes to the peace we do or don't receive from God. So if we only think on how things should change in order to get peace, we limit God to only giving us peace based on that circumstance. John 16:33 says, ***"These things I have spoken unto you, that in Me ye might have peace. In the world ye shall have tribulation: but be of good cheer; I have overcome the***

world." Jesus tells His disciples that they will have tribulations in the world, yet He tells them that He overcame the world. I believe He said this because if the disciples kept their mind on the promise Jesus made, it would give them peace. So why tell them they would have peace, but that in the world there would be tribulations? I believe He was trying to let them know that they wouldn't have peace just because the world was at peace.

Jesus wanted the disciples to know that they would have peace regardless of whatever situation they were in. John 14:27 says, ***"Peace I leave with you, My peace I give unto you: not as the world giveth, give I unto you. Let not your heart be troubled, neither let it be afraid."*** What the world gives is harmony, but that is based on everything being on one accord. However, Jesus told His disciples that He doesn't give like the world gives, which is circumstantial and situational, but what He gives is something divine called peace. In all of these examples, none of the situations have changed, yet in each instance, they have peace. That's why peace is so amazing because it's not a situational change, but a perspective change. This is why I know that if you aren't keeping your mind on Jesus' promises, you're the problem and not the situation. One of the meanings of peace is to be made whole, so peace means no division. The interesting part about this is that the word peace is a homonym for piece.

God will take the pieces in your life that you experienced when you didn't have peace and make you whole again.

That's because what we don't realize is that without peace, it is impossible to be whole or complete. John 5:6 says, ***"'When Jesus saw him lie, and knew that he had been now a long time in that case, He saith unto him, Wilt thou be made whole?'"*** The reason the man wasn't whole was because he lacked health in his body. This is why the body of Christ can be many members but one part, because God desires wholeness. 1 Corinthians 12:12 says, ***"For as the body is one, and hath many members, and all the members of that one body, being many, are one body: so also is Christ."*** God desires peace for His family (body of Christ) so that they can live more productive and effective lives for His use. When the whole body is whole, the whole body is at peace. Colossians 3:15 says, ***"And let the peace of God rule in your hearts, to the which also ye are called in one body; and be ye thankful."***

The Calm:

Another thing about peace is that it means that there is nothing threatening. 2 Chronicles 20:30 says, ***"So the realm of Jehoshaphat was quiet: for his God gave him rest round about."*** This was the difference between David and Solomon. In my mind, David would be the perfect person to build God's temple because he truly wanted to honor God by giving Him that sacred place to dwell in. However, 1 Chronicles 22:8 says, ***"But the word of the LORD came to me, saying, Thou hast shed blood abundantly, and hast made great wars: thou shalt not build an house unto My name, because thou hast shed much blood upon the earth in My sight."*** When God tells

David that He can't build His temple, it wasn't necessarily because he wasn't holy or clean. Since David was a man of war and shed blood, that also meant that there would always be a time he would be at war. If you're a king and trying to build anything, you know that means there is a chance of that building process being impeded.

God's temple was holy, therefore, it couldn't risk being destroyed because of an army's retaliation against David. So why Solomon? Not only did Solomon have wisdom, but God promised that He would give Solomon peace. 1 Chronicles 22:9 says, ***"Behold, a son shall be born to thee, who shall be a man of rest; and I will give him rest from all his enemies round about: for his name shall be Solomon, and I will give peace and quietness unto Israel in his days."*** God was very specific about what type of king needed to reign during the construction of the temple. Since Solomon was not at war with anyone, God gave the assignment to him. The rest that Solomon had was unlike what any other king had because it wasn't rest from sleep. Solomon's rest was peace with every surrounding nation. This is why he was able to be so prosperous in his time as king. Peace is what a lot of us are missing from our lives.

Most people are not able to get much done, let alone get rest to get things done, because they are worried about the potential of war. So again I say, when there is peace, there will be rest. Psalms 4:8 says, ***"I will both lay me down in peace, and sleep: for Thou, Lord, only makest me dwell in safety."*** The only way you sleep and have rest is when no one is threatening you. Rest is so important to God that He dedicated a whole day to it. Genesis 2:2-3 says, ***"And on the seventh day God ended His work which He had made; and He rested on the seventh day from all His work which He had made. And God blessed the seventh day, and sanctified it: because that in it He had rested from all His work which God created and made."***As we've discussed before, our peace is tied up in our rest. Rest is so important that God Himself did it first. He did this to demonstrate that all must rest from their work. Hebrews 4:9-11 says, ***"There remaineth therefore a rest to the people of God. For he that is entered into His rest, he also hath ceased from his own works, as God did from His. Let us labour therefore to enter into that rest, lest any man fall after the same example of unbelief."***

We can't keep trying to work and never rest, because we will never enter into God's rest. When we don't enter into His rest we won't experience His peace. However, when we stop working to make things happen, we enter His rest. His rest is a confidence that there is nothing more we could do because He has done everything. This doesn't always take effect on our jobs, but it most certainly affects us in our spiritual life. Going forward, we should stop thinking that our lives have to be perfect in order for us to have peace. No matter how our lives are, if we change our perspective, God will give us peace in all situations, at all times.

Ezekiel 34:25 says, ***"And I will make with them a covenant of peace, and will cause the evil beasts to cease out of the land: and they shall dwell safely in the wilderness, and sleep in the woods."***

YOU'RE THE PROBLEM... NOT MINISTRY Chapter 7.

John 13:15 says, ***"I have set you an example that you should do as I have done for you."*** In ministry, Jesus was not only commanding His disciples how to live, but He always showed them as well by doing what He commanded. The most important thing for us to consider is what example Jesus was setting for His disciples. If you read John 13:13-14, it says, ***"'You call me 'Teacher' and 'Lord,' and rightly so, for that is what I am. Now that I, your Lord and Teacher, have washed your feet, you also should wash one another's feet.'"*** Jesus acknowledged that what they called Him was true and that they were accurate in that they called Him Lord and Teacher. However, the example was not just His Lordship, but as a Teacher. He taught them how to fulfill their assignment in the earth realm so that they would also become leaders, but not lead as dictators.

Jesus showed them that He served, as a leader, so that they would become servant-leaders, who would lead and teach others how to serve through leadership as well. This is why it was important for Jesus to make sure that they saw Him serve, to get rid of the idea that His position was anything comparable to the Pharisees. Here lately, when some people get into ministry, they think status or titles give them the authority to lord over people. They look at it as an opportunity for others to serve and follow them, rather than them serve others and follow Christ. This had to have been the reason Jesus set the example that He did for His disciples in John 13:13-15. Ministry is defined as service to or serving others. Jesus' example to His disciples in washing their feet was that position in ministry doesn't mean others serving you, but that they would serve others.

The examples that Jesus set were like His recipes for ministry/discipleship and those recipes will work for us too! Before I say the recipe, I think it's important to look at the preparation process before you begin to follow the recipe. One of the most helpful things in cooking is prepping before you begin. You don't want to get started and have to keep stopping because you forgot something. The better you prepare, the better it will be following the recipe. One of the things Jesus did to prepare was to be baptized in water and by the Holy Spirit. Why? Well, Jesus knew He needed power in the flesh to do the things He was called to do. He also did it to set the example for the order of things in ministry.

When Jesus emerged from the water, Mark 1:9-13 says, ***"At that time Jesus came from Nazareth in Galilee and was baptized by John in the Jordan. Just as Jesus was coming up out of the water, He saw heaven being torn open and***

the Spirit descending on Him like a dove. And a voice came from heaven: "You are My Son, Whom I love; with You I am well pleased." At once the Spirit sent Him out into the wilderness, and He was in the wilderness forty days, being tempted by Satan. He was with the wild animals, and angels attended Him." Before Jesus ever went into ministry, He received the Holy Spirit. Why? Because Jesus was the example that in order for you to be able to handle ministry and all that comes with it, you need to be empowered.

You know that He received power because it says that after that, the Holy Spirit sent Him into the wilderness. However, being in the wilderness wasn't the problem. It was there that He fasted for 40 days and nights and being hungry, satan would tempt Him afterward. If Jesus didn't have the Holy Spirit, He wouldn't have had the power to have gotten past the first temptation, let alone all three! It was so important that Jesus took the time to prep (do the necessary things beforehand), because prep time is never lost time. If Jesus Himself needed power before going into ministry, what makes you any better that you wouldn't need the same? Jesus didn't need the Holy Spirit because He was weak. He received the Holy Spirit because He would be the Pattern. He was living out the steps of the recipe to show them that it would have the outcome He said it would.

Jesus knew that there would be things that they would encounter, that their natural man couldn't deal with. So He demonstrated that receiving the Holy Spirit would give them the power they needed to do what their assignment called for. This is not an assumption, but Jesus actually tells His disciples in Acts 1:8, ***"But you will receive power when the Holy Spirit comes on you; and you will be My witnesses in Jerusalem, and in all Judea and Samaria, and to the ends of the earth."*** Jesus made sure to emphasize not to go anywhere and minister before they received the Holy Spirit (power). After He received the Holy Spirit (power), His first assignment was not to jump right into the recipe, it was to continue in that prep time and preheat the oven.

If my mom were frying chicken, she would test the temp by dropping in a little flour to see if it is hot enough. If she were making cornbread, she didn't put the cornbread in first. She would put the oil in the pan and let it heat before putting in the cornbread mix. If she were making rice, she needed to boil the water first before adding the rice. All of these are examples of Jesus not jumping right into ministry before completing the prep time, which usually involved heat. After receiving the power of the Holy Spirit, it was put to the test in the wilderness (heat). After He passed that test, it was go-time!

Now that we've prepped, let's look at the recipe Jesus gave us for ministry and go from there. Jesus said in Luke 4:18-19, ***"The Spirit of the Lord is upon Me, because He hath anointed Me to preach the Gospel to the poor; He hath sent Me to heal the brokenhearted, to preach deliverance to the captives, and recovering of sight to the blind, to set at liberty them that are bruised, To preach the acceptable year of the Lord."*** Jesus was fully aware of His assignment and nowhere in this assignment did it say that He would be in this position to be served. At least not in that capacity.

So the recipe is:

1. Be anointed
2. Preach the Gospel to the poor (spiritually and naturally)
3. Heal the brokenhearted (spiritually and naturally)
4. Preach deliverance to the captives (spiritually and naturally)
5. Recover the sight of the blind (spiritually and naturally)
6. Set at liberty them that are bruised (spiritually and naturally)
7. Preach the acceptable year of the Lord

If you pay attention to what He said He was anointed to do, it was what He was anointed to do for others. If you aren't anointed, you will find it very difficult to do what follows ministry because nothing that follows has to do with anyone doing anything for you. Ministry is about how you can serve God by serving people and one of the most important things there is to ministering to others is telling them about the Good News (Gospel). They need to know that Jesus died for their sins, bought them with a price, and brought them back to a loving God. You also need to be anointed to heal broken hearts and to preach deliverance to those who are captive. If you aren't anointed to do these things, you will end up brokenhearted and in bondage.

When people don't have eyes to see, you have to help them to recover their sight just like Ananias did for Paul in Acts 9. Jesus was anointed to set free those who were bruised and the anointing on your life will not only help you to do this, but to proclaim the acceptable year of the Lord! When you see the recipe, although the outcome is an amazing product, what all goes into the recipe isn't all that glamorous. Jesus was going into places that were uncommon for most priests and doing things for those who people would otherwise not have helped! Everyone deserves the chance to hear the Gospel and from there make whatever decisions they will make of it. It's not on you what they decide, but it is on you to bring it to them for them to decide on.

Unfortunately, when we don't follow the recipe, a lot of us get burnout. This doesn't always happen because ministry is necessarily difficult or the people are hard to deal with, but it's because we try to do things in our natural power and do things we haven't been anointed to do! If you haven't received the Holy Spirit (power), it's going to be hard. If you aren't anointed for what you're doing, it's going to be difficult to do what you're doing. Even in all of this, Jesus has a recipe to get us back to the place we need to be. Jesus says in Matthew 11:28-30, ***"'Come unto Me, all ye that labour and are heavy laden, and I will give you rest. Take My yoke upon you, and learn of Me; for I am meek and lowly in heart: and ye shall find rest unto your souls. For My yoke is easy, and My burden is light.'"*** Let's look at this scripture in terms of a recipe.

Recipe:

1. Go to Jesus
2. Receive rest
3. Learn from Him (meekness and lowliness)
4. Being in service with Jesus is easy (better)
5. Task in service with Jesus is light (easy)

The first thing you have to do when you're feeling tired and burdened is to go to Jesus and receive from Him what you need. In this case, you need rest and relief. When you come to Him, He will first give you rest. After that He wants you to partner with Him (take His yoke) and learn His ways. By the way, His ways will teach you how to rest and not be burdened again in the future in ministry. He can give you something all day long, but if you never learn how to do it going forward, you will find yourself in cycles. Jesus teaches you that He is both meek and lowly in heart. Why is this important? Because if the Savior of the whole world doesn't have main character syndrome, but is meek and lowly, then you don't have any reason to be high minded.

Realizing that He didn't have to choose you and that in meekness and lowliness, you're almost guaranteed to be willing and obedient to do what He has called you to do, which is serve! This is how you get rest for your souls. Also, when you know that you are not doing it in your own strength and your humility tells you that all that you're doing, you need Jesus to do it, this too is how you find the rest that you need because you know it isn't you that's keeping you going! This is why we must learn this from Jesus because even He went to recharge by going into the secret place for long periods of time with God and being baptized with the Holy Spirit (power) before going into ministry.

If He didn't do those things, He Himself would've been worn out in the flesh. The same for you if you continue without humility and meekness. You will be in a state of unrest and burden because you will try to do these things without the help of Jesus. One very important thing about Matthew 11:28-30 is that it says, ***"and I will give you rest."*** Why is this so important? Well, I have either been around people or have been that person who was burnt out and had to take a pause. It almost makes you feel like God is giving you this hard task, with little to no strength to accomplish it! Have you ever said or heard someone say, *"I'm tired of ministry or I'm tired of the/this ministry"*? If you have, I guarantee you that there is a part of the recipe that you or they have not followed or omitted.

As much as rest is important to the longevity of ministry, partnering with Jesus is also important, because if you don't depend on Him to help you, that's when you get burnt out. Resting in and depending on Jesus is a real thing that we should do. Any burden or weariness we feel, Jesus wants us to be free of that so He could get more productivity in His Kingdom. Jesus also wants us to have balance. I will show you two examples of how it can be in ministry. Remember we talked about Jesus sleeping on the boat while the storm took place. Jesus wasn't up worrying or tarrying all night. No, He knew that He needed rest for the next ministerial assignment and He wants the same for you. On the contrary, Jesus also knew how to be refilled, even when it calls for you to not necessarily have natural rest. Luke 6:12 says, ***"And it came to pass in those days, that He went out into a mountain to pray, and continued all night in prayer to God."***

I am not a theologian, so I am not sure that every night He spent all night in prayer because when He was on the boat in the middle of the night, He was asleep. However, I do know He spent hours in prayer with God, not because He felt that was a requirement to be in ministry, but after spending all day with people, it was wisdom for Him to spend that time in prayer to commune with the Father, cast His burdens on Him and be rejuvenated. This was a good time to get strategy and make important decisions because the all night prayer mentioned in Luke 6:12 preceded Jesus choosing His 12 disciples. If spending that type of time with the Father was best for Jesus, it is also the best thing for us to do the same thing!

Jesus even understood that at times in ministry you will feel anxious and to some of our surprise, He knew what it was like to feel agony. Luke 22:44 says, ***"And being in an agony He prayed more earnestly: and His sweat was as it were great drops of blood falling down to the ground."*** No matter the anxiety or agony, Jesus continued to go back and forth to God in prayer because He was going to get confirmation of God's will for Him and it was where He was going to have to cast His burden in order to continue with His assignment. Let's look at the series of events that took place during Jesus time of agony in Matthew 26:36-45:

"Then cometh Jesus with them unto a place called Gethsemane, and saith unto the disciples, Sit ye here, while I go and pray yonder. And He took with Him Peter and the two sons of Zebedee, and began to be sorrowful and very heavy. Then saith He unto them, My soul is exceeding sorrowful, even unto death: tarry ye here, and watch with Me. And He went a little farther, and fell on His face, and prayed, saying, O My Father, if it be possible, let this cup pass from Me: nevertheless not as I will, but as Thou wilt. And He cometh unto the disciples, and findeth them asleep, and saith unto Peter, What, could ye not watch with Me one hour? Watch and pray, that ye enter not into temptation: the spirit indeed is willing, but the flesh is weak. He went away again the second time, and prayed, saying, O My Father, if this cup may not pass away from Me, except I drink it, Thy will be done. And He came and found them asleep again: for their eyes were heavy. And He left them, and went away again, and prayed the third time, saying the same words. Then cometh He to His disciples, and saith unto them, Sleep on now, and take your rest: behold, the hour is at hand, and the Son of man is betrayed into the hands of sinners."

Jesus went three times to petition God about His crucifixion, but soon after gained strength in His Presence. He took that sorrow and agony to God and was able to get it off of Him. 1 Peter 5:7 says ***"Cast all your anxiety on***

Him because He cares for us". Jesus demonstrated this recipe when He began to cast His cares on God. God doesn't desire that we be anxious or exhausted just to say we've ministered. He wants us to cast whatsoever issues we help carry for others on Him so that we can be good for the next assignment. If not, that's when we feel burdened. Another thing is, Jesus was very honest about His feelings, because that's the only way God can deal with your issues. I like to say, God can't bless a lie, so why do you lie to God, expecting Him to answer that lie?

Prep Time Requires Patience:

Another point to make about ministry is that a lot of people know that they are called in ministry in some shape or form, but the problem that most have is not their willingness, but their patience. Just because God has called you to ministry, answering the call doesn't mean that your assignment starts right then. 1 Samuel 16:12-13, ***"And he sent, and brought him in. Now he was ruddy, and withal of a beautiful countenance, and goodly to look to. And the Lord said, Arise, anoint him: for this is he. Then Samuel took the horn of oil, and anointed him in the midst of his brethren: and the Spirit of the Lord came upon David from that day forward. So Samuel rose up, and went to Ramah."*** What is interesting about this is that although David was anointed king, he didn't actually reign as king until years later.

We know this because David was anointed king before he slew goliath and we know that David was still young because Saul called him a boy before the battle in 1 Samuel

17:33. However, 2 Samuel 5:4 says that David wasn't actually king until he turned 30 years old. So when Samuel anointed David king, what was he doing the whole time? Serving! Not just serving, but patiently serving! That's the part that a lot of ministers miss is that although they may have been called or anointed, they want to operate in the now with gifts that God is preparing for later. The recipe was there and David was cooking up a masterpiece! Before we look at the serving, let's look at the patience. We never see that David complained about how long it took for him to become king.

From slaying goliath, to serving in the army, to playing the lyre for Saul, David served without any recorded impatience or complaint. I think David understood that God was going to be faithful to His Word, so no matter how long it took, he was going to wait patiently for it. Romans 8:25 says, ***"But if we hope for that we see not, then do we with patience wait for it."*** This means that David had an expectation that it would happen, so when the recipe called for him to wait patiently for it, he did just that. If a minister refuses to wait and decides to go ahead and step out and do things out of God's timing, they will feel the heavy burden and the difficulty of the yoke. What do I mean? If God told you it's about to rain and that He will come back with an umbrella, but you had to wait for it, what would you do?

What if that umbrella represented His covering of protection? Some ministers are so impatient that they would rather get wet and endure unnecessary hardship, rather than waiting. Whenever ministers do that, you are putting more on yourself than God requires of you. As a matter of fact, you are putting more on to do in your own strength, than God required of you! When this happens, for some strange reason, people blame God and being in ministry, rather than their own impatience. God tries to prepare you because if we go too soon, we will encounter things we won't know how to deal with and it could harm us.

Acts 19:13-16 says, ***"Then some of the traveling Jewish exorcists (men who adjure evil spirits) also undertook to call the name of the Lord Jesus over those who had evil spirits, saying, I solemnly implore and charge you by the Jesus Whom Paul preaches! Seven sons of a certain Jewish chief priest named Sceva were doing this. But [one] evil spirit retorted, Jesus I know, and Paul I know about, but who are you? Then the man in whom the evil spirit dwelt leaped upon them, mastering two of them, and was so violent against them that they dashed out of that house [in fear], stripped naked and wounded."*** If you notice, it says they tried casting out demons in the name of Jesus whom Paul preaches. These are those in ministry that were too impatient to take them time to get the same Jesus Paul had and learn of Him.

If God is saying wait, He is not trying to hinder us, He is trying to help us avoid things we don't have to experience without Him. Instead of these ministers being patient and preparing for what was coming, they got themselves in a situation where they were whooped up on. Was that God's fault? No! Was it because they were in ministry? No! God will not call you to something you aren't prepared for. However, some ministers will overlook their faults and blame the ministry, as if the ministry is full of setups! The best thing you can do during that waiting period is to prepare. This is one of the reasons why when I attempt to do a recipe, I still mess up because I don't account for the prep time. Proverbs 24:27 says, ***"Prepare your work outside; get everything ready for yourself in the field, and after that build your house."*** When you do things out of order, you are bound to have some hiccups along the way.

One time there were some virgins who didn't prepare for the bridegroom and when he came, they couldn't go with those who did. So what does preparation time look like? Serving! I don't care at what time and no matter who you are or what you've done, there is no way to skip over serving in ministry, because that is what ministry is! This goes back to one of Jesus' initial recipes for ministry. Before He walked in His anointing, He served. Jesus is the Blueprint! Although we could also reference David or Joseph, I want to point out one person who is not often discussed in this category (possibly because he has a rather troubling start to his calling) and that's Jacob. Before Jacob became the father of the twelve tribes, his first ministry was marriage. He was told he had to serve 7 years for his wife and he did. Genesis 29:20 says, ***"And Jacob served seven years for Rachel; and they seemed unto him but a few days, for the love he had to her."***

Jacob was so in love with his first ministry (Rachel), when he was deceived into marrying her sister, he patiently served another 7 years for Rachel. **Sidebar: Sometimes, our patience is challenged, because we don't always love the ministry God has called us to enough to wait patiently for it. Jacob's love helped him wait patiently for what God had for him.** Not only was Jacob patient, but he prepared by serving his father-in-law until his time came. Jacob wouldn't have had all the possessions he needed to provide for his family on his own, so he had to continue to serve until it was time for him to begin his next ministry as overseer of his whole family and their possessions. He would've definitely been burdened with the responsibility and everything would have been difficult for him and his family if he didn't serve and ultimately gain provision and possessions to lead a family.

As ministers, we can't grow impatient and not prepare, because when our time comes, we will be too burdened because we didn't prepare to carry the load that we forced on ourselves for going into ministry before time. We will also be embarrassed because our time came and we were not ready.

To God and Not Unto Man

Another thing that is a part of the recipe that a lot of people mess up on is only seeing that you are serving people and not seeing that you are serving God by serving people. The thing that hinders so many people in ministry is not just burnout or impatience, but offense. People get offended or they refuse to continue because they take offense at the people or at the idea of serving people. One of the things I think that helped Jesus and has definitely helped me (when

I am able to humble myself and think clearly) is Colossians 3:23 says, ***"And whatsoever ye do, do it heartily, as to the Lord, and not unto men; Knowing that of the Lord ye shall receive the reward of the inheritance: for ye serve the Lord Christ."*** Whenever I think like this, it's harder to become offended, because my service is not unto man, but to God! I am only trying to please the Lord at that point and if I am thinking about doing my best to make sure I serve the Lord with excellence, I see less of the person and more of Jesus.

If the person is someone I don't really care for, gets on my nerves, or is rude, my service is still not as difficult if I think about the fact that I am pleasing God by being obedient to serve in the capacity He has asked of me! A scripture that most people like is Ephesians 6:5-8, because it says, ***"Servants, be obedient to them that are your masters according to the flesh, with fear and trembling, in singleness of your heart, as unto Christ; Not with eyeservice, as menpleasers; but as the servants of Christ, doing the will of God from the heart; With good will doing service, as to the Lord, and not to men: Knowing that whatsoever good thing any man doeth, the same shall he receive of the Lord, whether he be bond or free."*** Most people associate this scripture with slavery or that it condones slavery.

Contextually, this was a servant who was probably in debt and having to serve off what they could pay. I am not using it for either case, but for the fact that as ministers, we are servants and we are called to serve the Lord Jesus. In doing so, we are trying to catch the eye of the applause of man, but of God, because He rewards us. If in ministry I am doing God's will when I am serving God's people from the heart if I am serving them well. Remember what I said about loving God's ministry makes you patient, but love makes you serve well also! 1 Corinthians 13:5 says love seeketh not her own or in the New International Translation, it says love is t self-seeking. In ministry, we should not just seek to serve God, but to do it from the heart (love it!).

Being called a servant or serving in ministry doesn't make me less than, but it makes me great in the Kingdom of God! Matthew 23:11 says, ***"But he that is greatest among you shall be your servant."*** If we are patient, prepared (serving), and serve unto God and not unto man in ministry, we could be the example that other ministers need as to how to get the desired results in ministry. Who knows, it could have been Jacob's patience and servant-leadership that influenced the patience and servitude of Joseph. Either way, God has given us all the recipe for ministry so none of us have the excuse of a failed product.

Galatians 6:9 says ***"And let us not be weary in well doing: for in due season we shall reap, if we faint not."***

You're The Problem, Not...

Quantity Chapter 8.

God wants us to all be saved. That means there are multitudes of people that He wants to not only receive His salvation, but also be in His family. However, God has never needed the multitude to make any of this or anything to happen. If we look at the beginning of time, God started with Himself to create the universe. When I say Himself, I mean the Trinity (Father, Son, Holy Spirit) and they discussed making mankind in Their image. Did I mention that mankind includes a large number of people? One man and one woman were used to expand humanity and when things went left (so many times), God used one family to start over. Lastly, God made a covenant with one man and his seed, that He would cause nations to come from.

Although there are so many examples of God using a few, sometimes we forget and convince ourselves that we need a multitude to get more done. We must be reminded that God doesn't need much to make a lot happen. If you are starting a business, a single parent, or trying to complete a task, the amount of people you have or don't have won't be the reason you can't accomplish it. As a matter of fact, if you think like this, your mindset will be the greatest hindrance to any progress you're trying to make. God has given us all a purpose and everything we need to accomplish that purpose is on the inside of us. 2 Peter 1:3 says, ***"According as His divine power hath given unto us all things that pertain unto life and godliness, through the knowledge of Him that hath called us to glory and virtue:".***

Knowing that we have everything we need to accomplish our purpose, it is important that we seek God for the wisdom and guidance as to how to pursue and ultimately fulfill that purpose. Although this is true, so many of us have yet to start, because we are too busy looking around at who isn't there to help us or what we don't have. I've used the man at the pool of Bethesda as an example before, but I will use him again to make this make sense. For 38 years, or at least for the majority of his life, he was never made whole, because he focused more on what someone wouldn't do for him, instead of what he was able to do for himself. His mindset crippled him more than his physical condition.

Jesus wasn't for the pity party. He gave him some life changing advice that I think we all need to hear. John 5:8 says, ***"Jesus saith unto him, Rise, take up thy bed, and walk."*** Jesus' advice was simple, quit waiting on others to help, DO IT YOURSELF! When we change our mind, we thrust ourselves out of a place called eventually, and into a place called immediately. John 5:9 says, ***"And immediately the man was made whole, and took up his bed, and walked: and on the same day was the sabbath."*** How far along could the man have been if he realized that everything he needed to be made whole, he already had. How much have we missed out on because we've been waiting on God to give us more. For some, God is saying do it yourself. For others He is saying, use who and what you already have. Either way, God wants you to stop making excuses and get it done! If in the beginning God created everything from nothing, you don't have an excuse!!!

I want to make sure we make all of this valid by backing this up by scripture. Genesis 1:27-28 says, ***"So God created man in His own image, in the image of God created He him; male and female created He them. And God blessed them, and God said unto them, Be fruitful, and multiply, and replenish the earth, and subdue it: and have dominion over the fish of the sea, and over the fowl of the air, and over every living thing that moveth upon the earth."*** God took two people and multiplied the number of humans that would come from them. So why do you think you need 20 people to start the business? What if God is saying He only wants to start with you and your spouse or you and your business partner? Oh, I get it! You're too busy looking at that corporation of people and you feel little in their eyes.

If you feel intimidated, let me remind you that every tree you see started from a seed. The same with every corporation, they started with just a few people with a vision and grew and developed to the place they are today. What if God can do more with the two of you than the multitude of people?! 1 Samuel 14:6 says, ***"And Jonathan***

said to the young man that bare his armour, Come, and let us go over unto the garrison of these uncircumcised: it may be that the LORD will work for us: for there is no restraint to the LORD to save by many or by few." When Jonathan went on a sneak attack of a huge army, he convinced his servant that nothing would stop God from saving His people, whether he used the whole Israelite army, or just the two of them. God doesn't need a lot of you to do anything. He just needs those who are willing and obedient to start and He will do the rest through you!

Quality Over Quantity:

I believe God will never do anything that would make us trust in something we don't need. God often uses quality rather than quantity because He knows that if He allows us to think that He needs quantity (not quality), then man would trust in numbers and not God. David got in a lot of trouble about counting the number of men in His army, because God never wanted him to feel like the number of men he had was the cause of his victories. God's way of doing things usually looks the exact opposite of the world's way of doing it, which for most people looks backwards. 1 Corinthians 1:27 says, ***"But God hath chosen the foolish things of the world to confound the wise; and God hath chosen the weak things of the world to confound the things which are mighty;"***.

God's path for Joseph to save his family looked really different compared to the way the world would've done it, so I'm sure a lot of people would've seen his path as foolish. The world's way would have been to make

Joseph's dreams come true by making him the head over his family because of talent or intellect. Well, Joseph's road to becoming second in command was anything but that. He was hated on and almost killed by his brothers, sold into slavery, lied on, falsely imprisoned, forgotten about and THEN remembered, lauded, and promoted to second in command. Joseph said of his path in Genesis 45:7, ***"And God sent me before you to preserve you a posterity in the earth, and to save your lives by a great deliverance."*** The plan that Joseph's brothers thought would kill him, was the one God used to save them.

God could've used all of Joseph's brothers to save the nation of Israel, but He only used one. This way, no one could take credit for saving God's people, but God Himself! Joseph had a quality about himself that none of his brothers had. That's what made God choose just one instead of all his brothers. Of course, Jesus was the perfect example of quality over quantity. He didn't come in the form of a giant or a mythical creature. He came in the form of a man, feeling and tempted by all that we are tempted with, yet He did not sin. God would use this one Man to save the world. Why? It was the quality of the man that allowed Him to do what the quantity of men could not. Jesus was put in this position because in the Old Testament, priests had to offer up so many sacrifices to atone for the sins of the people.

The sacrifices became irrelevant because people began to bring lame sacrifices and since the priest couldn't even get it right, the sacrifices never saved man from his sinful nature. Nothing that man was doing ever brought them back into relationship with God, so something or Someone of quality, had to replace this method. It didn't need to keep happening multiple times, but one time to take care of it forever. 1 Peter 3:18 says, ***"For Christ also hath once suffered for sins, the Just for the unjust, that He might bring us to God, being put to death in the flesh, but quickened by the Spirit:".***

I know you're probably thinking that it was easy for God to find quality in Jesus, because it's Jesus. However, there were other men in the bible that God saw quality in that He knew He could use rather than a multitude of men (quantity). Joshua 23:10 says, ***"One man of you puts to flight a thousand, since it is the Lord your God who fights for you, just as He promised you."*** God's power isn't shown through using the multitude to save the few, but God always demonstrates His power by using the few to save the multitude. We already established that God only sent Jesus to save the world from their sins, but we should also pay attention to how much He did in a short amount of time. Out of His 33 years of living, He only needed 3 years to fulfill His purpose and only 3 days to conquer death, hell, and the grave. This is very impressive to say the least.

What's also impressive is how God used a small group of people to rebuild what was destroyed. In the Old Testament, God's people were sent into exile because of their constant disobedience. During the time of the exile, the city and the holy temple were destroyed. After 70 years, God allowed His people to come back, but when they did, they had to do a lot of work to repair the city, the temple, and the walls (for protection). According to Bibleask.org, *"The rebuilding of the Temple from the day the Jews laid its foundation stone for the second time (Kislev 24, 2d year of Darius) to its finish, had therefore taken about 4 years and 3 months. This period was about 2 years and 3 months less than it had taken King Solomon to build the first temple."* This means that the remnant (small remaining quantity) that God brought back from the exile did in a shorter amount of time what a larger group of skilled workers did in a longer amount of time!

Of all the people who went into exile, God used the remnant from the exile to build back up His nation. Jeremiah 23:3 says, ***"Then I will gather the remnant of My flock out of all the countries where I have driven them, and I will bring them back to their fold, and they shall be fruitful and multiply."*** For those who knew that the remnant of Israelites would eventually go back and try building back up their nation, I'm sure it was puzzling how they were going to accomplish that great task with so few people. But again, God never needed a large number to accomplish what He purposed.

Although this was very impressive, Jesus had something more impressive that He would accomplish in 3 days. He said to the Jews in John 2:19-21, ***"Jesus answered and said unto them, Destroy this temple, and in three days I will raise it up. Then said the Jews, Forty and six years was this temple in building, and wilt thou rear it up in three days? But He spake of the temple of His body."*** God didn't need 33 years to rebuild the body that Jesus had. What they tried to kill, God raised up in 3 days! In God's wisdom, He wouldn't allow for the story to end once Jesus was resurrected and seated at the right Hand of the Father. Before He completed His mission, Jesus recruited a dozen disciples to further expand the Gospel. John 14:12 says, ***"Verily, verily, I say unto you, He that believeth on me, the works that I do shall he do also; and greater works than these shall he do; because I go unto My Father."***

Jesus promised His disciples that they would do greater than Him after He left and it didn't take a multitude to do it! After Jesus' disciples received the Holy Spirit, Peter addressed a crowd of people outside of the upper room. Acts 2:41 says after people finished speaking, ***"Then they that gladly received His Word were baptized: and the same day there were added unto them about three thousand souls."*** 120 people started out in the upper room, but 3,000 people were added. From that day, the disciples went out and discipled others until the Gospel spread throughout the world!

Many Are Called, Few Are Chosen:

I said all of this to say that we have no excuse for why we can't accomplish what God has given us to do in this earth realm. Many people blame their lack of productivity on the lack of people they have to help them. What if you can't get it done because of the amount of people you are trying to add to your team. God is not going to use anything that can get His credit and He doesn't need your many to make you mighty. In Judges 7:2, it says, ***"And the Lord said unto***

Gideon, The people that are with thee are too many for Me to give the Midianites into their hands, lest Israel vaunt themselves against Me, saying, Mine own hand hath saved me." God tells Gideon straight up why He felt that way about using a lot of men in his army. He didn't want Israel's army to think that their size, and not the Hand of God, saved them.

God had Gideon reduce his army down to an uncomfortable number and made him go into battle like that. Psalms 33:16 says, ***"No king is saved by the size of his army; no warrior escapes by his great strength."*** When God had Gideon lessen the number, their victory was undeniably won by God. This is another example of why God uses the remnant to save His people. Your thoughts have to be, well if this is all I have, then I know God will do the rest! He wants you to have the same confidence in Him to save you as He does in saving you. This is why God hasn't given it to you. It's not because of the amount of people you don't have, but due to the amount of people you do have. God would rather take a few qualified people to bring about His will, than a multitude of unqualified people.

Matthew 22:14, ***"For many are called, but few are chosen."*** You may have in mind a bunch of people, but God will get down to the one person who will give Him the glory, before He takes a group of arrogant people. When Jesus was on His way to raise Jairus' daughter from the dead, it said He only took Peter, James, John, and the parents of the little girl, in the room where she was. I don't think it's by coincidence, because when they got to the man's house, Mark 5:39-41 says, ***"He went in and said to them, "Why all this commotion and wailing? The child is not dead but asleep." But they laughed at Him. After He put them all out, He took the child's father and mother and the disciples who were with Him, and went in where the child was. He took her by the hand and said to her, "Talitha koum!" (which means "Little girl, I say to you, get up!")"***

I believe Jesus only would allow those around Him who had faith enough to believe, which is why He put out an entire room of mockers and only kept her parents and three of His disciples. I also believe He only took those three disciples because at one point Jesus told His disciples that they had little faith. Everyone can't go into places with you that require great faith because they don't all have the faith to believe it will happen. Usually only a few out of the multitude will believe. God will eliminate those who will hinder the miraculous from happening in your life.

Doing A Lot With A Little:

Provision is definitely one of those examples of how God can use a little to do a lot. When Jesus fed the multitude using only two fish and five loaves, He was showing the people that He can provide for their needs with what they had. As amazing as this was, I can understand why Jesus got frustrated when the disciples thought that He was concerned about providing food for them on another occasion. Matthew 16:8-11 says, ***"Which when Jesus perceived, He said unto them, O ye of little faith, why***

reason ye among yourselves, because ye have brought no bread? Do ye not yet understand, neither remember the five loaves of the five thousand, and how many baskets ye took up? Neither the seven loaves of the four thousand, and how many baskets ye took up? How is it that ye do not understand that I spake it not to you concerning bread, that ye should beware of the leaven of the Pharisees and of the Sadducees?"

Jesus was basically saying, how could you think that I was talking about providing for y'all?! Think about it, why would Jesus not be able to provide for 12 if He provided for the multitude? Jesus didn't need much to provide for the large crowd, so providing for that small number of people was nothing for Him. Out of all of these examples, people will still complain today that lack limits them. It's really not lack, but our perception of what the world says we need for something to happen vs. what God says we need. Our problem is that we like to blame what we can't do on how much we have or don't have, but scripture dispels that every time with how God used individuals or small groups of people to do much with little, especially Jesus!

Matthew 25:22-23, ***"He also that had received two talents came and said, Lord, thou deliveredst unto me two talents: behold, I have gained two other talents beside them. His lord said unto him, Well done, good and faithful servant; thou hast been faithful over a few things, I will make thee ruler over many things: enter thou into the joy of thy lord."*** However, if you're making excuses with the little you have, God can take that and give it to someone who will do more with it. Matthew 25:24-28 says, ***"Then he which had received the one talent came and said, Lord, I knew thee that thou art an hard man, reaping where thou hast not sown, and gathering where thou hast not strawed: And I was afraid, and went and hid thy talent in the earth: lo, there thou hast that is thine. His lord answered and said unto him, Thou wicked and slothful servant, thou knewest that I reap where I sowed not, and gather where I have not strawed: Thou oughtest therefore to have put my money to the exchangers, and then at my coming I should have received mine own with usury. Take therefore the talent from him, and give it unto him which hath ten talents."***

It's not how much, but how you're using what you have. Another aspect of quantity is the amount of money you have. So many times we think the lack of money is what hinders us from doing more. However, sometimes the more money you have hinders you from doing more, because the problem was never with the amount of money you had. The problem is the person who had that amount of money. In Luke 16:1 it says, ***"And He said also unto His disciples, There was a certain rich man, which had a steward; and the same was accused unto him that he had wasted his goods."*** A lot of us are not good stewards of our money, therefore, more money would never solve our problem. The idea that because we don't have more money is the reason we don't have more is the mindset of a person who will never get ahead no matter how much money they have.

Why? Well the question is not what will you do with the more money you receive, but what did you do with the least amount of money you had to begin with. He had one chance to get it right before going to his master, so he had to shift the way he was thinking in order to get different results. Luke 16:10 says, ***"He that is faithful in that which is least is faithful also in much: and he that is unjust in the least is unjust also in much."*** If you haven't made good money decisions with the little you have, why would you think you would be able to handle more? Think of this analogy, if I lift weights and I can barely lift 10bs, why would I ask for 20 lbs to be added on? It wouldn't be wise to add more to what you can't handle. As a matter of fact, it's dangerous!!! God knows that it's dangerous to add more money to a person who can barely handle the least, the same way it's dangerous for someone to add more weight to someone's bar who can barely lift the least amount of weights they have already.

The more you get, if you're unfaithful, the more damage you have to make. Jesus goes on to say in Luke 16:11, ***"If therefore ye have not been faithful in the unrighteous mammon, who will commit to your trust the true riches?"*** If you took out a loan and didn't manage that money well, why would the bank give you more to mismanage? This is the same for those who want more responsibility. If you can't manage the little responsibility, more responsibility will just overwhelm you! Luke 16:12 says, ***"And if ye have not been faithful in that which is another man's, who shall give you that which is your own?"*** The steward, obviously, was someone in authority because he was over the rich man's goods. He wasn't judged on what he did with his own stuff, but what he did with someone else's.

If you lack anything, don't blame anything or anyone else, anymore. Rather, look around you and see what it is that you have and how you're managing it. If you aren't responsible with what you have, and you aren't given more, as a result of it, just blame yourself. We have to start seeing that there is a problem with how we're handling what we have as the primary reason we have been blocked from having access to more. This goes for what you manage for yourself and what you manage for others. If you don't know how to handle being a boss for someone else's organization, don't start a business. As a matter of fact, why would you want more responsibility, when what you have is overwhelming you? You will have more responsibility to mess up!

We also have to stop with the idea that God doesn't want us to have more as to why we don't have more. John 10:10 says, ***"The thief cometh not, but for to steal, and to kill, and to destroy: I am come that they might have life, and that they might have it more abundantly."*** The deception is that God doesn't want you to have more, but the truth is, He wants you to have it abundantly, but the right way! God wants us to live the abundant life, but not a life that is wasteful of the abundance that He has given us. So the lie is that God doesn't want us to have more, but the reality is we can't handle the more that He wants to give us. Most times people have not because they do not ask, according to James 4:2. However, most of us are asking. Not just asking, but asking God for more! Here's the thing, some of us that are asking for more, are asking because we want more for ourselves.

Unlike the reason before, God isn't giving it to you because you will mismanage it, but because your motive is wrong! James 4:3 says, ***"Ye ask, and receive not, because ye ask amiss, that ye may consume it upon your lusts."*** The Amplified Classic translation of James 4:3 says, ***"[Or] you do ask [God for them] and yet fail to receive, because you ask with wrong purpose and evil, selfish motives. Your intention is [when you get what you desire] to spend it in sensual pleasures."*** God doesn't mind you having what you asked for, if what you asked for isn't for you only. He doesn't even mind you having more, if the more will be used for the right reasons. Also consider that if you have one gift and you're messing over that, why would God reveal other gifts to you?

Your one gift is enough if you use it well. 1 Peter 4:10 says, ***"As each has received a gift, use it to serve one another, as good stewards of God's varied grace:".*** It's not going to be how many gifts you have, but how you use the gift you have. Proverbs 18:16 says, ***"A man's gift maketh room for him, and bringeth him before great men."*** It doesn't say how many gifts make room for him and bring him before great men, but his gift (singular). If you're using your gift to serve others, God says this makes you a good steward. We know that those who are good stewards are those that receive more to steward over. The more God is able to trust you with what you have, the more God can give you.

Matthew 25:21 says, ***"His lord said unto him, Well done, thou good and faithful servant: thou hast been faithful over a few things, I will make thee ruler over many things: enter thou into the joy of thy lord."***

You're The Problem, Not...

Friendship Chapter 9.

Let me say this loud and clear before I start. I AM NOT SAYING YOU'RE THE ONE WHO HAS CAUSED THE DAMAGE IN THE FRIENDSHIP. If you've gotten this far in the book with me, I think you know that I am making a point that we both can agree on. This chapter is no different. Ok, now that we have that out of the way, let's continue. Failure in friendship can be caused by one or both parties involved, depending on the lack of mutual investment. However, if you're the one investing and the other is not, wouldn't that mean that they're the problem? Partially. I say that because, since we can't control others, it's best that we focus on ourselves. Looking at it through a self-reflective lens, the failure of a friendship is based on what type of friend you are, the type of friend(s) you attract based on who you are, or the type of friend(s) you accept. What do I mean? Let's first start off with looking at the type of friend you are.

One major detail to the recipe is found in Luke 6:31, which says, ***"And as ye would that men should do to you, do ye also to them likewise."*** Simply put, treat others the way you want to be treated. We stimulate good friendships when we treat the other person in the friendship the way that we desire or expect them to treat us. The success of it comes when it is reciprocated. If you want them to be loyal to you, be loyal to them. If you want them to be a supportive friend, show up and support them. If you want to be respected, respect your friend as well. Respect in friendship sets a standard that either the other will rise to in order to keep the friendship, or will fall short of it and lose the friendship. One example of this is Job and his friends. Job was experiencing one of the lowest seasons of his life and to make matters worse, the entire time his friends criticized him rather than comforted him. All he wanted were friends who would treat him the way he would've treated them if they were in the same situation.

Job 16:1-5 (NIV) says, ***"Then Job replied: "I have heard many things like these; you are miserable comforters, all of you! Will your long-winded speeches never end? What ails you that you keep on arguing? I also could speak like you, if you were in my place; I could make fine speeches against you and shake my head at you. But my mouth would encourage you; comfort from my lips would bring you relief."*** We have to be mindful not to be the type of friends who respond in ways that are contrary to the way we want to be treated. Although Job's friends treated him opposite of how he would've treated them, that type of behavior didn't go unnoticed by God.

Job 42:7-9 says, ***"After the LORD had said these things to Job, He said to Eliphaz the Temanite, "I am angry with you and your two friends, because you have not spoken***

the truth about Me, as My servant Job has. So now take seven bulls and seven rams and go to My servant Job and sacrifice a burnt offering for yourselves. My servant Job will pray for you, and I will accept his prayer and not deal with you according to your folly. You have not spoken the truth about Me, as My servant Job has." So Eliphaz the Temanite, Bildad the Shuhite and Zophar the Naamathite did what the LORD told them; and the LORD accepted Job's prayer." God made it very clear to Job's friends that He did not like the way they handled the situation and it would take a sacrifice and Job's prayers for God to not cause them to be in the same situation as Job.

If you are the type of friend that Job had, let me warn you now, your friendship is not only in trouble, but it will get the attention of God! God wants us to have friendships that are based on love. This doesn't mean that if you see your friend doing wrong that you overlook it just to comfort them in their sin. It means that even if you are holding your friend accountable, our response should be in love. Proverbs 17:17 says, ***"A friend loveth at all times, and a brother is born for adversity."*** Be the type of friend that loves your friend through the good and the bad. Whether you're comforting or correcting your friend, let it be done in love, treating them the way you want to be treated. Jonathan handled his friendship better than Job's friends. Not only did Jonathan love his friend at all times (Proverbs 17:17), but he loved him as he loved himself!

1 Samuel 18:1-2, which says, ***"After David had finished talking with Saul, Jonathan became one in spirit with***

David, and he loved him as himself. From that day Saul kept David with him and did not let him return home to his family." To love someone as you love yourself is indicative of the fact that you treat others the way you want to be treated. Part of the reason Jonathan and David's friendship was so successful was because they treated each other the way they wanted to be treated and it was done in love. For some people, the concept of friendship seems too good to be true or that real friendship does not exist. However, we should consider the people we choose to be in friendship with as one of the reasons for our failed results.

2 Corinthians 6:14-18 says, ***"Be ye not unequally yoked together with unbelievers: for what fellowship hath righteousness with unrighteousness? and what communion hath light with darkness? And what concord hath Christ with Belial? or what part hath he that believeth with an infidel? And what agreement hath the temple of God with idols? for ye are the temple of the living God; as God hath said, I will dwell in them, and walk in them; and I will be their God, and they shall be My people. Wherefore come out from among them, and be ye separate, saith the Lord, and touch not the unclean thing; and I will receive you. And will be a Father unto you, and ye shall be My sons and daughters, saith the Lord Almighty."***

Whenever we've heard verse 14 of this chapter, we automatically think of marriage. That's a good association, however, this is applicable to any relationship we are establishing. We shouldn't be in any type of relationship that does not edify us or that we can't edify someone else in return. Relationships of any kind (friendships, companionships, partnerships, etc.), especially Godly relationships, must be both reciprocal and mutual in the same way it is explained in Proverbs 27:17, which says, "***Iron sharpeneth iron; so a man sharpeneth the countenance of his friend.***" If we are choosing to be in fellowship with individuals who are not sharpening us and we are the ones who are not sharpening them, we can't be upset with the outcome of a dull, meaningless friendship.

I understand that most people we call our friends don't necessarily have the same mindset or morals that we do, but they are fun to be around. Unfortunately, that still isn't sufficient enough to be in friendship with anyone! I believe the only way you can truly get reciprocation in friendships, is being friends with those who are like-minded. It never tells us that Jonathan knew David prior to David defeating Goliath, but it does tell us his initial encounter with David after having met him. It wasn't what David said to Jonathan that prompted the way that he responded to David. I believe it was the fact that Jonathan saw someone who was like him. He also saw someone who was brave, fearless, and trusted in God.

We know this because 1 Samuel 14:6 says, "***And Jonathan said to the young man that bare his armour, Come, and let us go over unto the garrison of these uncircumcised: it may be that the LORD will work for us: for there is no restraint to the LORD to save by many or by few.***" If David was brave enough to fight Goliath on his own and Jonathan prior to that was brave enough to go into the enemy's camp with just the young man who carried his armor, they had some things in common. They also had in common that they both wanted to destroy the enemy that disrespected God and threatened His people. I am imagining that in that first conversation that Jonathan was privy to, he must have found someone of like faith and character.

If we want healthy friendships, we must be yoked with those who share the same mindset as us. Unfortunately, some people are equally yoked in a negative way. If both you and your friend have Godly character and believe the same things, you are equally yoked. This means you both move in the same direction and have a fruitful friendship. However, what happens if you and your friend are both toxic and negative? It means that you are negatively equally yoked. If you come to realize that you and your friend have similar negative characteristics, you may want to take the time to ask yourself what is attracting these people to you or attracting you to them, and then work on those things.

I am not saying that if you have a bad friendship it is always your fault, but you have to at least be open to looking within yourself. Why? Because when you learn to look inside yourself before we look outside yourself, you may discover there was something inside of you that contributed to the failure of that friendship. Galatians 6:7 says, ***"Be not deceived; God is not mocked: for whatsoever a man soweth, that shall he also reap."*** Imagine this in friendship. If you're unsupportive, you may get unsupportive friends. If you're rude and disrespectful, you may get that back in your friendship. You can't reap anything if you don't sow first. Neither can you get good fruit if you sow bad seeds. Therefore, if your fruit is always bad in friendships, maybe you should check the seeds that you sowed!

Fear Blocks Friendships:

In order to sharpen each other, you can't be worried if you sharpen your friend, they may be sharper than you. If this happens, you will be too intimidated to sharpen the person as much as they sharpen you, because you will be afraid that they will be better than you! I heard a pastor say this about my pastor once as it pertained to being his friend, *"Either you can be intimidated or you can be inspired."* The pastor said that he chose to be inspired! As for Jonathan, I truly believe that he was inspired by David. Unfortunately, a lot of people aren't inspired in the friendships they are developing or already have established. Instead, they allow the enemy to trick them into comparison, which breeds insecurities in the friendship.

I think this is another way we go wrong in the recipe for friendship. Oftentimes we allow our insecurities to make us intimidated of our friends, which causes us to not want to help them, especially when we know that it will help them. Intimidation is synonymous to and grounded in fear. Therefore, we let fear keep us from an amazing friendship. 1 John 4:18 NIV says, ***"There is no fear in love. But perfect love drives out fear, because fear has to do with punishment. The one who fears is not made perfect in***

love." Jonathan knew that David succeeding didn't mean he was failing. Therefore, he considered David's success as his own success as well! Fear is what keeps us from doing one of the things that Jesus commanded us in John 15:12-13 NIV, ***"My command is this: Love each other as I have loved you. Greater love has no one than this: to lay down one's life for one's friends."***

I think what Jonathan and David had in common allowed Jonathan to see and love David as himself. He saw someone who was willing to risk their life for their God and their nation like he would. 1 Samuel 18:3-4 says, ***"And Jonathan made a covenant with David because he loved him as himself. Jonathan took off the robe he was wearing and gave it to David, along with his tunic, and even his sword, his bow and his belt."*** Jonathan saw that David gave his best. I believe this inspired Jonathan so much that he was willing to give his best to ensure that David didn't lack anything that would make him successful.

Disclaimer: I am not saying that you have to give people things in order to establish your friendship or love for them. No, not at all! I don't believe Jonathan was trying to buy David's friendship. I think that Jonathan set the tone for their friendship. Job 6:14 says, *"Anyone who withholds kindness from a friend forsakes the fear of the Almighty."* **David didn't start out as a soldier and definitely wasn't wealthy, so he came in with nothing. I believe Jonathan was communicating to David that because I love you as a friend, I will not withhold good**

from you that will help you get better. He was willing to share what he had to make sure that David succeeded from that point forward.

Unfortunately, Saul, Jonathan's dad, wasn't inspired by David because he became intimidated by him. That intimidation of David only exposed Saul's insecurities. From there, he began to do what some people do in friendships, which is secretly (and sometimes openly) try to destroy the person they are intimidated by. Saul tried to have Jonathan assist him in his plan to kill David, but he wasn't the type of friend that wanted to see his friend's demise. Instead, he was going to help David. 1 Samuel 20:30-31, ***"Then Saul's anger was kindled against Jonathan, and he said unto him, Thou son of the perverse rebellious woman, do not I know that thou hast chosen the son of Jesse to thine own confusion, and unto the confusion of thy mother's nakedness? For as long as the son of Jesse liveth upon the ground, thou shalt not be established, nor thy kingdom. Wherefore now send and fetch him unto me, for he shall surely die."***

If Jonathan was intimidated by David, he would've set him up to be killed just to ensure he would be heir to the throne. Not that Jonathan was willing to die for David, but him being willing to save David, even if that meant him giving up his chance at becoming king, is a type of "lay down your life for your friend" situation! Since Jonathan loved David as a friend, he would demonstrate one of the key components of the recipe for Godly friendships, loyalty. As a result of Jonathan's loyalty, some relationships were going to be compromised. One of the relationships that would be compromised was the one between him and his own dad.

Loyalty is Key:

One of the things I know that God will do when you follow the recipe for Godly friendships, is expose the problem and the solution. I know this may seem very small, but another thing my mom was serious about in her recipes were brands. In her opinion, sometimes certain brands made her cakes' outcome change. Why? Because sometimes the off brand may have had to compensate by having an additional ingredient or a slightly different amount of something that the original brand had. Sometimes you pay more for the name brand because of the name. However, there are other times you pay more for the name brand because of the quality! If my mom knows a name brand has the best results, she will remain loyal to that brand, no matter the cost. Very few times has she had to use the generic brand, but whenever she did, she normally regretted it.

My mom's loyalty to the brand, in her opinion, was worth the price. For Jonathan, his loyalty to David may have cost him a lot, but he knew it was worth the cost. He also knew that following the recipe for Godly friendships by being loyal to David would not only give the nation great results, but would also give him the desired outcome. In 1 Samuel 20:15, Jonathan and David made a covenant, which says, ***"But also thou shalt not cut off thy kindness from my house for ever: no, not when the LORD hath cut off the enemies of David every one from the face of the earth."***

We will see later on how Jonathan's loyalty to their friendship didn't just affect him, but it also affected those connected to him. Unfortunately, Saul's disobedience affected those connected to him as well. Saul sought a woman who had a familiar spirit of Endor, to seek counsel from Samuel, who was deceased.

1 Samuel 28:19 says, ***"Moreover the LORD will also deliver Israel with thee into the hand of the Philistines: and to morrow shalt thou and thy sons be with me: the LORD also shall deliver the host of Israel into the hand of the Philistines."*** As a fulfillment of a prophetic word from the Lord, through the prophet Samuel (who was deceased), Jonathan and his brothers died in battle with their dad Saul. Although Saul's disobedience caused him and his sons to lose their lives in battle, the good thing is, David didn't forget the covenant that he and Jonathan made. 2 Samuel 9:1 says, ***"And David said, Is there yet any that is left of the house of Saul, that I may shew him kindness for Jonathan's sake?"*** The people told David about Jonathan's son, Mephibosheth. So, David sent for him. 2 Samuel 9:7 says, ***"And David said unto him, Fear not: for I will surely shew thee kindness for Jonathan thy father's sake, and will restore thee all the land of Saul thy father; and thou shalt eat bread at my table continually."***

Loyalty is so important to the success of friendships, that it has lasting effects! As a result of Jonathan's loyalty, David kept his covenant to Jonathan, even though they made that covenant years prior! One of the reasons anyone can remain loyal is because of trust. Lack of trust can affect how deep your friendship can go. Proverbs 18:24 says, ***"A man that hath friends must shew himself friendly: and there is a friend that sticketh closer than a brother."*** A lot of us have used this one way, but when I read other translations, I learned something different. The NIV translation says a man with unreliable friends comes to ruin. Again, not having trust in friendship will eventually ruin the friendship. Are you a trustworthy friend? Do you befriend unreliable friends? Well, we shouldn't blame anyone but ourselves for the results we're getting, because these are not traits that produce successful friendships!

I also understand loyalty and trust can be compromised when there are too many people involved to be loyal to or trust. A lot of people talk about how their circle is small, maybe because they don't trust people. This can be a response from hurt, but I like to believe that having a small circle isn't always a bad thing. Another translation of Proverbs 18:24 says a man with many companions comes to ruin. Why? Again, I think this deals with trust, because it's hard being loyal to or trusting too many different personalities. If you are the type that thinks you have to have a lot of friends, you may end up disappointed in the end. I will discuss this again later, but out of the multitude, Jesus only went with 12 disciples and in very intimate situations, He only went with 3. Why? Because He knew He couldn't trust everyone with every situation.

Discern The Bad, But Still Let It Work For You

When Jesus told His disciples to follow Him, it wasn't because He was looking to have a good time. He was so intentional about His assignment to them, which was building them up for their assignment for the Kingdom of God. It was a mutual relationship that both benefited from. The only person you saw around Jesus that wasn't on the same type of time He was on, was Judas. Unfortunately, but also fortunately, Judas had to be there because He played a very crucial role in the prophecy being fulfilled. Psalms 41:9 says, ***"Yea, mine own familiar friend, in whom I trusted, which did eat of my bread, hath lifted up his heel against me."*** Contrary to what Judas may have thought, he wasn't a surprise to Jesus, because he already discerned who he was. This is why discernment is so important to all relationships, especially friendships, because you don't want to be around people who genuinely don't have your best interest at heart!

The wrong friendships will be like what we saw happen with Jesus! They will mask their true intent in order to be in fellowship with you, only to betray you in the end. Proverbs 27:6 says, ***"Faithful are the wounds of a friend; but the kisses of an enemy are deceitful."*** Their motives are hidden behind the guise of being supportive, so they can remain close by for easy access to you. However, God gives us the discernment to be able to recognize it and call it out like Jesus did. If you aren't quite sure about it, that's when you have to ask God for wisdom to be able to discern who you should be in fellowship with and who you shouldn't. James 1:5 says, ***"If any of you lack wisdom, let him ask of God, that giveth to all men liberally, and upbraideth not; and it shall be given him."***

God allows us to have enough warnings to know who we shouldn't have a friendship with. This is a bit of a sidebar, but God can still use those bad friendships too. Think about it, Judas had to happen because the story of redemption would be nothing without opposition. I heard this guy say in a song something like, *"What is the good without the bad?"* It may not have been said exactly like that, but the point is, it makes what Jesus did mean and feel so much more intense. We also gain wisdom moving forward after those bad experiences, but let's be honest, who really wants to gain wisdom like that? Not me! Therefore, it is best that we stay sensitive to the Holy Spirit in our friendships, because if we pay attention, He gives us those warnings before we make a commitment to be in the friendship.

If you went to buy a car you wouldn't buy it without test driving it first to see if it is suitable for you, would you? We shouldn't do friendships like that either. 1 John 4:1 says, ***"Beloved, believe not every spirit, but try the spirits whether they are of God: because many false prophets are gone out into the world."*** God gives us the ability to test these friendships out just like we would a car. If we are wise and discern the warnings, we avoid bad situations. However, if we ignore them, we may end up with a "lemon" (bad investment) of a friend. Sometimes we ignore warnings and it catches up with us in the end. I don't know why we choose to blame everyone and everything else in those moments when we decided to ignore what the Holy Spirit was trying to show us.

When we choose to go into friendships without allowing God to reveal to us if it is a healthy friendship or not, we suffer unnecessary frustration as a result. Not only that, we also walk away from these friendships worse than when we started. This is because we often pick up bad habits and spirits from those we shouldn't be in fellowship with. Proverbs 22:24-25, ***"Make no friendship with an angry man; and with a furious man thou shalt not go: Lest thou learn his ways, and get a snare to thy soul."*** We have to stop allowing ourselves to be around people who live contrary lives to those we know God has called us to live. The only reason we sometimes tolerate bad friendships is because of the potential or hope of change. This is when we put on our superhero cap and make the mistake of thinking that we can change people.

The truth of the matter is that we don't change people, God does! We either sow the Word or water the Word that has been sowed (by us or others), but bringing that change to pass is God's job. Paul tells us in 1 Corinthians 3:6-7, ***"I have planted, Apollos watered; but God gave the increase. So then neither is he that planteth any thing, neither he that watereth; but God that giveth the increase."*** Another hard truth to accept is that God did not call us to everyone. Galatians 6:2 tells us to bear one another's burdens, but this isn't the same as you trying to save someone. In their ignorance, you are there to help, minister, and encourage them, with the Word of God. However, once we've done everything God told us to do, He wants the burden of saving the person on Him, not on us. John 12:32 says, ***"And I, if I be lifted up from the earth, will draw all men***

unto me." Jesus didn't even give us the burden of drawing others to Him. He said He would do the drawing Himself!

Jesus, the Model Friend:

If there were a blueprint for friendship, of course it would be Jesus. Although He could have, Jesus didn't allow His disciples to only serve Him. He demonstrated the balance and humility He desires in our friendships by serving them as well. What I love is that Jesus didn't come out the gate calling the disciples His friends. There were things that He needed to see in them to determine if they deserved that honor of being called friend. Sometimes we are too quick with giving someone that honor of being called friend without seeing if they possess those characteristics. At the right time, Jesus explained what it meant to be His friend and what it meant for Him to be theirs. Again, John 15:14 says, ***"Ye are My friends, if ye do whatsoever I command you."*** Most of our friendships are based on what people do for us or what we do for people and if that doesn't happen, the friendship is in jeopardy.

Jesus wasn't telling His disciples that they could only be His friends if they did what He said. I think it was more so Jesus saying that He is teaching them right from wrong and doing what is contrary to that makes their friendship unequally yoked. What was it that Jesus was commanding them to do? Jesus tells them in John 15:12-13, ***"This is My commandment, That ye love one another, as I have loved you. Greater love hath no man than this, that a man lay down his life for his friends."*** Jesus gave a command to His disciples, but He wasn't bossing them around to do something He wanted them to do in order to benefit Himself. He commanded them to love others in friendship as He demonstrated His love in friendship to them. This wasn't based on selfishness like most people in one-sided, dictating friendships. Jesus explained to them a friendship that consisted of selfless acts, based on love.

Jesus always demonstrated first what He wanted us to do. Not only did He show His friendship in the way that He loved them, but He also showed how He loved others. So, loving Jesus is continuing to spread that love to all that He loves. Jesus was able to sum up what friendship to Him is, that if they operated in their friendship in this manner, this made them His friend. I also loved that Jesus showed how to be wise by trying every spirit by the Spirit when it came to friendships. He operated in discretion until He knew He could trust them with His business/secrets. John 15:15 says, ***"Henceforth I call you not servants; for the servant knoweth not what his lord doeth: but I have called you friends; for all things that I have heard of My Father I have made known unto you."***

When it comes to friendships, it is wise that if you have not established a friendship with someone, you shouldn't just tell all of your secrets. Jesus didn't share those secret things that He heard from His Father with the crowd or with the religious leaders. As a matter of fact, He spoke to everyone in parables. Jesus even spoke in parables with His disciples until He knew whom He could trust or whose spirit proved to be in agreement with His. John 16:25 says, ***"These things have I spoken unto you in proverbs: but the time***

cometh, when I shall no more speak unto you in proverbs, but I shall shew you plainly of the Father." Jesus was going to stop speaking in parables and speak plainly, but not to everyone. He only gave this honor to those who were in covenant with Him, which were His disciples. Mark 4:33-34 says, ***"And with many such parables spake He the Word unto them, as they were able to hear it. But without a parable spake He not unto them: and when they were alone, He expounded all things to His disciples."*** Jesus was a Gatekeeper of the secrets and mysteries of God, because they weren't just for everyone to have.

The disciples began to notice that Jesus at one point only spoke in parables to everyone else, except them and they wanted to know why. Matthew 13:10-16 NIV says, ***"And the disciples came, and said unto Him, Why speakest Thou unto them in parables? He answered and said unto them, Because it is given unto you to know the mysteries of the Kingdom of heaven, but to them it is not given. For whosoever hath, to him shall be given, and he shall have more abundance: but whosoever hath not, from him shall be taken away even that he hath. Therefore speak I to them in parables: because they seeing see not; and hearing they hear not, neither do they understand. And in them is fulfilled the prophecy of Esaias, which saith, By hearing ye shall hear, and shall not understand; and seeing ye shall see, and shall not perceive: For this people's heart is waxed gross, and their ears are dull of hearing, and their eyes they have closed; lest at any time they should see with their eyes and hear with their ears, and should understand with their heart, and should be***

converted, and I should heal them. But blessed are your eyes, for they see: and your ears, for they hear."

The things that Jesus knew and heard from God couldn't be told to just anyone, because either people don't believe or they use things against you. God only reveals things to those He knows are His. Deuteronomy 29:29, ***"The secret things belong unto the LORD our God: but those things which are revealed belong unto us and to our children for ever, that we may do all the words of this law."*** The way Jesus handled His friends versus His acquaintances, is the type of wisdom God wants us to operate in with our friendships. That is because everyone does not know how to handle your secrets. When people wonder why I am so private, my response is because people don't know what to do with my business. Meaning, if they don't pray for what they hear, they can't handle what is personal to me.

You have those "friends" who will take your information and spread it, under the guise of being concerned. They will even have the audacity right before gossiping to say, *"We need to pray for them, because..."* and by the time they've told all your business, they never actually prayed for you! Proverbs 17:9 advises that, ***"He that covereth a transgression seeketh love; but he that repeateth a matter separateth very friends."*** Your business should not be a topic of conversation for others, but rather, a prayer point. James 5:16 says, ***"Confess your faults one to another, and pray one for another, that ye may be healed. The effectual fervent prayer of a righteous man availeth much."*** So-called friends who gossip about your business are either secretly happy about what you're going through because they are not your friends at all, or they want to be entertained. On the contrary, real friends that pray for you want to see you delivered/healed from that situation.

This doesn't happen with just any regular person you encounter. This has to be someone who wants to see good come to you so much so that they discipline themselves to only speak to God about you and not gossip to others. This is why everyone wasn't privy to Jesus' business like that! Jesus operated in such discretion that He handled His information as a great honor to discover. Proverbs 25:2 says, ***"It is the glory of God to conceal a thing: but the honour of kings is to search out a matter."*** Jesus concealed the secrets to the Kingdom of God because it was only for those whom He considered kings and queens. Commoners wouldn't handle this type of information as an honor, that's why it's not for them to seek it! This is why Jesus says in Matthew 7:6, ***"Give not that which is holy unto the dogs, neither cast ye your pearls before swine, lest they trample them under their feet, and turn again and rend you."***

People won't always handle with care what you value! It was the honor of His disciples and those who were given the privilege to seek out the knowledge of the Kingdom of God. Therefore, the more they sought, the more He revealed to those He could trust. Some people try to get into friendships because of what they can get from the other person without giving anything back. This is not to say that you should look for things from your friend. However, you are looking for reciprocity in how well you treat/respect your friends. Proverbs 14:20 says, ***"The poor is hated even of his own neighbour: but the rich hath many friends."*** The rich man doesn't have many friends because he or she is so amazing, but they have something people want. The poor man isn't hated because he is a bad man, but because he or she doesn't have anything to offer those people. They chose not to be friends of the poor person because those who handle people like that aren't their real friends, but they are opportunists. Therefore, the friendship doesn't last because if you're a good friend and they aren't, it's not going to last long because there is only output and no input.

The rich man will be treated the same way as the poor man if the rich man were to lose all his money! We have to ask God for discernment to know who is truly for us and who is not. Earlier we talked about asking yourself what was on the inside of you that attracts the type of friends you have or what attracts you to the people you are in friendship with. Well, one of the last things to ask yourself is, "W*hat type of people do you attract?"* Have you ever heard the saying, *"Opposites attract?"* I believe this can be true, because opposite charges attract. Although this can be true, I think we should be very careful with this. Why? Because some people will give themselves this excuse to get into friendships with people who are bad influences, if they themselves are good or vice versa. Think about it like this, if one person is a believer and the other is not, someone will be converted. 1 Corinthians 15:33 says, ***"Do not be misled: "Bad company corrupts good character."*** So if this opposite only sows into you things that are bad, it will eventually corrupt you.

If there is an opposite in friendship, it needs to be that they are strong in the area you are weak in and the area they are weak in, you should be strong in. The only way opposites work is when you have two individuals who, although they are opposites, use that to make the other person better. Proverbs 13:20 says, ***"He that walketh with wise men shall be wise: but a companion of fools shall be destroyed."*** If you aren't wise, but walk with the wise, with the intention of becoming wise, chances are, you will become wise. On the contrary, befriend a foolish person, who doesn't want to become wise from your wisdom, if you walk with them, you will be destroyed as a result. Real friends will help lift the other to a place where they have fallen. Ecclesiastes 9:9-10 says, ***"Two are better than one; because they have a good reward for their labour. For if they fall, the one will lift up his fellow: but woe to him that is alone when he falleth; for he hath not another to help him up."***

Whether you're attracting friends who are opposite of you or you attract friends with the same character, it must be to make the other better to glorify God. If not, that friendship may not last or won't bring God glory! Let's keep in mind all of the recipes that we may have failed at with friendship and try to follow them step by step so that we can get very different, yet desirable results.

Luke 6:31 says, ***"And as ye would that men should do to you, do ye also to them likewise."***

You're The Problem, Not...

Marriage Chapter 10.

MARRIAGE IS NOT BAD, but you can have bad forms of marriage if there is a failed execution of the recipe. Even if one person is the only one following the recipe, if the other person is not following the recipe as well, the recipe is still not being followed. The recipe for marriage should model what scripture gives us as the blueprint, Christ and the Church. Anything contrary to this is a failed execution of the recipe. I will speak more to Christ and the Church later, but a lot of times in marriage, we confuse, not so much as the role, but the assignment of the husband and the wife. From the very beginning God had unity on His mind. Genesis 1:26-27 says, ***"Then God said, "Let Us make mankind in Our image, in Our likeness, so that they may rule over the fish in the sea and the birds in the sky, over the livestock and all the wild animals, and over all the creatures that move along the ground. So God created mankind in His own image, in the image of God He created them; male and female He created them."***

When God created Adam, it wasn't just Adam and Eve He was creating, but all of mankind. When God created mankind, He created them in His image. To take it a step further, He had in mind a union, called marriage between male and female. Their purpose was to have a relationship with God, each other, and also populate and have dominion in the earth. Genesis 2:18 NIV, ***"The LORD God said, "It is not good for the man to be alone. I will make a helper suitable for him."*** God was very specific in how He desired these roles to go, whether it's our relationship with mankind, but definitely our relationship between husband and wife. Although God was specific about it, somehow things are getting lost in translation as to how things should be or how things should happen in a union. When this happens, or rather continues to happen, it begins to pass down more confusion to each generation until His intent is no longer clear.

I give this disclaimer often when I speak to anyone who is still married, *"I am divorced, so I can't tell you how to keep your marriage, because I couldn't keep mine."* So I am never trying to give you information that I've either never applied or didn't work for me. What I will say is, *"I am divorced and I can tell you what could lead to a divorce."* What do I mean? Hindsight is 20/20 and I've had time to think about, not my marriage in particular, but God's intent for marriage and whether my marriage aligned with that. Revelations 12:11 says, ***"And they overcame him by the Blood of the Lamb, and by the word of their testimony; and they loved not their lives unto the death."*** The point I am trying to make here is that testimony, with the Blood of the Lamb, helps people to overcome. So I can testify to a lot of things that can help some people overcome. I had three different perspectives about marriage before the Lord gave me the revelation He gave me.

My first perspective was that I sincerely believed that I would get remarried and my desire was to be married to someone who was serious about not just our marriage, but also about the things of God. My second perspective came when I began to go through these very angry and disappointed emotions. I began to think that I didn't even want to be married anymore, because people seem to not be serious about marriage or not using their marriage to glorify God. My last perspective was that marriage wasn't what I thought it was and maybe, just maybe it never could reach the standards of what the Word of God said it should because, let's be real, we are dealing with very flawed humans. Therefore, in my mind, no one really has that type of exemplary marriage. I felt like no matter how happy people looked, there was always a lie behind closed doors.

Disappointment and hurt will do that to you. It will rob you of your optimism and leave you only with negativity. Proverbs 13:12 NIV, ***"Hope deferred makes the heart sick, but a longing fulfilled is a tree of life."*** This was the place I probably was at the longest, with only a few times hoping that this new reality I had wasn't true. I can honestly say I understood what hope deferred felt like because I hoped for God to "fix" my marriage for so long. When I got a divorce, my heart was not sick, but it was completely over the thoughts of marriage working. This wasn't solely based on my experience, but I've learned that people can skew your beliefs by their actions and your experiences with them. So, I took my experience and the experiences of those around me and made up in my mind that it would never and could never be the way God said it was in the Bible. At that point, I concluded that this was the experience of the people in the Bible, and that it would not occur again.

Whew! I was having some "woman scorned" responses during that time in my life and it wasn't anything cute about it. Until one day, on July 30, 2022, God gave me a revelation about marriage. It was as if I was having this conversation with someone and listening to people complain about marriage not working. Then, the Holy Spirit spoke to them through me and said, *"People give up on marriage thinking it doesn't work, but it's because they don't work in marriage."* When the Holy Spirit said that, that thing gave me one of the biggest "Aha" moments I've had in a long time! I said, *"God, that's it!"* It's not marriage, because you've made it perfect! It's so perfect that it was one of the institutions you started with and the one in the book of Revelations, Christ will demonstrate in the end.

Revelations 21:2 says, ***"And I John saw the holy city, new Jerusalem, coming down from God out of heaven, prepared as a bride adorned for her husband."*** So how could marriage be the problem? Better question, could the problem actually be the people in marriage? It's a humbling and sobering thought, but the answer is yes! Hebrews 10:35-37 says, ***"Cast not away therefore your confidence, which hath great recompence of reward. For ye have need***

of patience, that, after ye have done the will of God, ye might receive the promise. For yet a little while, and He that shall come will come, and will not tarry." A lot of times we lose confidence (faith) because we either lose patience with doing God's will or we don't do His will at all. When this happens, we don't get the promise and we assume that it was never going to happen to begin with. This causes us to think that God isn't a God of His Word, when really, we aren't men and women of our word. Instead of reevaluating ourselves, we reevaluate the institution of marriage. Marriage is supposed to represent who Christ is to the Church.

If we understood what marriage represents, then we wouldn't doubt it. So for those who don't understand, they doubt. In order to behold our faith (confidence), I think we have to start with the basics of what marriage is and why it was instituted. Genesis 2:18 says, ***"And the LORD God said, It is not good that the man should be alone; I will make him an help meet for him."*** It doesn't specifically say this, but for God to create anything on the earth, it was because He wanted it. Think about it, if we are created in the image of God and He Himself has never been alone (God the Father, the Son, and the Holy Spirit), He wouldn't create us to be isolated either. More importantly, God created man because He obviously wanted the relationship with mankind, as well as, share His creation with us.

Relationship is one of the things that we have in likeness with God. Since we are made in the image of God, the same way God is not alone, He wouldn't allow us to be alone either. Therefore, He gave man a help, because it wasn't good that he (Adam) or any man (and all mankind) to be alone. God actually created the male and female before He ever discussed their union. He created the male and female in Genesis 1:27, but there had not been conversion about their union yet. So, when God made the women in the flesh, marriage was implemented. Genesis 2:24 says, ***"Therefore shall a man leave his father and his mother, and shall cleave unto his wife: and they shall be one flesh."*** In Their (Father, Son, and Holy Spirit) individuality, there is oneness in the Triune God. God has also called us to be one with Him as well. When man and woman marry and consummate that marriage, they are no longer seen as two individuals, but as one. Genesis 5:2 says, ***"Male and female created He them; and blessed them, and called their name Adam, in the day when they were created."***

When God called them Adam, He was speaking to the oneness of the two. This oneness was created in the image of what God created, meaning marriage is supposed to replicate the marriage of Christ and His bride, the Church. Ephesians 5:30-32 says, ***"For we are members of His body, of His flesh, and of His bones. For this cause shall a man leave his father and mother, and shall be joined unto his wife, and they two shall be one flesh. This is a great mystery: but I speak concerning Christ and the church."*** From marriage man and woman's consummation should be the avenue to multiply the earth. I remember this couple who spoke at a marriage seminar at my church called, *"After we say I DO"*, they related the husband to

Christ and how the woman has characteristics of the Holy Spirit. I will look at two verses that exemplify that statement. The first is in John 14:26, where Jesus said, ***"But the Comforter, which is the Holy Ghost, whom the Father will send in My name, He shall teach you all things, and bring all things to your remembrance, whatsoever I have said unto you."***

In the New King James translation, the Holy Spirit is called the Helper. God said that He would create a help meet suitable for Adam. God also promised to send the Holy Spirit, which is called the Helper. The second scripture is Romans 8:26, which says, ***"Likewise the Spirit also helpeth our infirmities: for we know not what we should pray for as we ought: but the Spirit itself maketh intercession for us with groanings which cannot be uttered."*** The wife is the help to her husband and the Holy Spirit was sent to us as our Helper. See the correlation? For the husband, Ephesians 5:25 says, ***"Husbands, love your wives, even as Christ also loved the church, and gave Himself for it;".*** If we look at the character of Christ and the Holy Spirit, it gives us insight to what our character should be as a husband and as a wife.

Ephesians 5:25-27 say, ***"Husbands, love your wives, even as Christ also loved the church, and gave Himself for it; That He might sanctify and cleanse it with the washing of water by the Word, That He might present it to Himself a glorious church, not having spot, or wrinkle, or any such thing; but that it should be holy and without blemish."*** Christ as a Husband, waters His church with the Word, which keeps her holy, producing this beautiful display, that doesn't look neglected or lacking. All of these are good characteristics to have, but in order for any of this to bear fruit, husbands and wives should be the expression of the image that we were created in.

Honor and Respect:

How you treat each other in a marriage is so important. Unfortunately, due to a lot of misinterpretations of the Word of God, husbands and wives don't treat each other well. Beginning with the husband, Ephesians 5:28 NIV says, ***"In this same way, husbands ought to love their wives as their own bodies. He who loves his wife loves himself."*** We communicate with our actions all the time. When you don't love your wife, you're not communicating how you feel about her, but how you feel about yourself. I heard Joyce Myers say once, *"You can't give what you don't have."* A husband lacking self-love couldn't give his wife the type of love Christ required for her because he is void of love for himself. For instance, if a guy didn't have love expressed to him as a child, he may lack that sensitivity to his children and/or his wife.

If he was told that boys don't cry, instead of expressing to others that his heart is broken, those suppressed emotions may come out in other unhealthy ways. The tough love that he was shown as a child is the only way he knows how to express love to his wife, but this love is communicating the opposite intention to her. I am not a counselor, nor am I trying to be, but I think we fail young boys when we deem the expression of love as a weakness. Love, built on the foundation of the Word of God, cultivates healthy relationships for both men and women, especially in marriage. If there is no input of this, we can't expect any output. Another important factor in treating each other well is knowing that leading doesn't mean the wife doesn't deserve her husband's respect. The Word of God definitely tells the wife to submit to her husband, but nowhere does it say that the wife has to be subservient. God did not give the husband dominion over his wife, but a great amount of responsibility in making sure she is cared for and protected. Somewhere, this translates to most men as dishonoring the woman.

1 Peter 3:7 says, ***"Likewise, ye husbands, dwell with them according to knowledge, giving honour unto the wife, as unto the weaker vessel, and as being heirs together of the grace of life; that your prayers be not hindered."*** Sometimes men assume because they are the head of the wife, he is superior to or better than her. However, he must honor her as the weaker vessel. The Amplified Classic Translation tells us that the word weaker is referring to her being physically weaker. This does not mean she is weak as in not to be valued or honored, because remember it says they are heirs together for the grace of life. Here's the thing, they are husband and wife. The husband is the head of the wife, but they are brother and sister, equal in Christ. The man won't get more of an inheritance than the woman, because he is the head. No, they both inherit together. If you decide to dishonor your wife, it doesn't matter how much you pray, there will always be a hindrance to those prayers being answered.

On the other end, the wife should honor and respect her husband as well. She shouldn't make this hard for him, because he assumes responsibility for her. When I say responsibility, I am not talking about work. I know that a greater majority of women are employed and not homemakers. What I mean is that God holds him responsible for his household. When God created a woman, He said she would be a help to him, not competition. We all understand that women are in the workforce now and can still carry the torch of being wife and mother, but that doesn't mean you treat him insignificantly. Nowadays, some women like to flex that they don't need a man. Well, that's cool, I guess. However, if you plan on reproducing, whether with or without a husband, you actually need something from a man. I would like to put an end to the argument that "I do not need a man" because it is not entirely true.

By the way, if you are married and this is what you're telling your husband, that is officially a failed recipe. Proverbs 18:22 NIV says, ***"He who finds a wife finds what is good and receives favor from the LORD."*** Women get hype about this verse, but most don't understand what this means. If all you bring him is drama, unnecessary stress, and pressure, did he really find a good thing? Or should I say, if the wife is a good thing to her husband, what would you call it if all she does is bring him the opposite of good? I'll let you answer that for yourself. I can be honest and say I knew what the Word (recipe) said and did the complete opposite, so I am not surprised by the results. **Disclaimer: I**

will also say that there is an element of my divorce that did not deal with any form of disrespect to a man, but to God. That's a long story that I won't get into right now. So back to the regularly scheduled program. The truth is, in order for any of us to see the desired results, we can't rely on anything other than God's Word.

Wives should treat their husbands the way the Word of God tells them to and not be influenced by single or unmarried women lyrics. That is absolutely no knock on any of them, because heck, I'm single, so clearly I have things I know I need to work on. I said that because if their lyrics are encouraging you to do something contrary to what the Word of God says about marriage, your results will be disappointing. Proverbs 31:12 NIV says a virtuous woman, ***"... brings him good, not harm, all the days of her life."*** Unfortunately a lot of women talk to men like they are children. I am not trying to be mean, but that is not what the Word of God tells us we should do. Wives should honor their husband's position as head over her life as she would her boss.

You fear repercussions of being insubordinate to your boss on your job, but do you fear what God says will happen if you dishonor your husband. David's wife thought it was cute to try to check David about his actions after bringing the ark of the covenant back to Israel. 2 Samuel 6:20-23 says, ***"Then David returned to bless his household. And Michal the daughter of Saul came out to meet David, and said, How glorious was the king of Israel to day, who uncovered himself to day in the eyes of the handmaids of***

his servants, as one of the vain fellows shamelessly uncovereth himself! And David said unto Michal, It was before the LORD, which chose me before thy father, and before all his house, to appoint me ruler over the people of the LORD, over Israel: therefore will I play before the LORD. And I will yet be more vile than thus, and will be base in mine own sight: and of the maidservants which thou hast spoken of, of them shall I be had in honour. Therefore Michal the daughter of Saul had no child unto the day of her death."

This is not to say that God would cause you to be barren if you got smart with your husband one time. This is a good example of how you can shut down your own blessings, due to dishonor and disrespect.

Family:

As I said before, marriage is a ministry. When it comes down to your family, it is the first ministry you have. How you do with that ministry will determine if He can trust you with a ministry outside of that. Marriage wasn't just designed for us to live with someone for the rest of our lives and have children, but it is to teach us the different levels of our relationship with the Godhead. Family, not just marriage, is one of the best pictures of the Godhead's relationship with mankind. Don't believe me? Let me show you. I will first start with marriage. Marriage is the example of Who Christ is to the Church. This is why when Matthew 22:30 NIV says, ***"At the resurrection people will neither marry nor be given in marriage; they will be like the angels in heaven."*** We will have no need of the example of marriage anymore, because we will experience and fully understand it firsthand. That is like someone keeping the sample when they've received the product. The sample is irrelevant at that point!

When we get married, we are having or supposed to have a natural, physical, and earthly experience of what our relationship should be with Christ and the Church. This is the Bridegroom and His bride. We are supposed to understand as Christ's Bride (the Church) the depths of His love for us. When the wife experiences love from the husband and the husband understands how to give that love to his wife, he is taught first hand how he should operate as a husband. This is because he is given an example by the Husband, Jesus. Notice I didn't say from God, the Father. We will discuss that example when we discuss parenting.

Understanding Order:

A recipe is not about just following the steps, but following them in order. Why? Because certain things won't happen if they are not followed by each other. For example, if you have a cake and you need the baking soda to react with the citric acid, but you put water, egg, and milk before the citric acid, chances are, it won't turn out the same. Before the wife can submit to her husband, her husband must first submit to Christ. 1 Corinthians 11:3 NIV says, ***"But I want you to realize that the Head of every man is Christ, and the head of the woman is man, and the Head of Christ is God."*** Although Jesus is a member of the Godhead, even He has a Head over Him, which is God. Jesus couldn't lead without submitting. Why would God ask Him to lead, if He didn't first understand how to submit? If He didn't submit to God, how could Jesus understand those He would have to live among?

Jesus gives the recipe of leadership in Matthew 20:25-28 NIV, ***"Jesus called them together and said, "You know that the rulers of the Gentiles lord it over them, and their high officials exercise authority over them. Not so with you. Instead, whoever wants to become great among you must be your servant, and whoever wants to be first must be your slave— just as the Son of Man did not come to be served, but to serve, and to give His life as a ransom for many."*** If anyone wants to be great, guess what, their position is not predicated on how bossy and dictating they can be, but on how well they serve. The husband isn't trying to marry so he can get a lifetime slave, but it's to demonstrate to his wife the same love that was first demonstrated to him. What does that love look like? Not him being served all the time, but him serving his family.

Some of the examples of Christ's servitude are feeding the hungry, washing His disciples feet, traveling to heal the dead (not saying that he has to travel to try to heal the dead, but this is an example of being selfless), and the list goes on and on. So, if a husband expects to be served well, he must also serve well. There is seed in your service. The husband's seed is how he submits to Christ and his harvest is in how his wife submits to him. The husband can only learn this by submitting to Jesus. In today's society, if a husband openly told someone that he leads his family as a servant leader, most people would look at him like he was weak. However, Christ never looked at His acts of service as something that made Him weak, but what would make Him great. Paul tells us the recipe for Christ greatness!

Philippians 2:5-11 NIV says, ***"In your relationships with one another, have the same mindset as Christ Jesus: Who, being in very nature God, did not consider equality with God something to be used to His own advantage; rather, He made Himself nothing by taking the very nature of a servant, being made in human likeness. And being found in appearance as a man, He humbled Himself by becoming obedient to death— even death on a cross! Therefore God exalted Him to the highest place and gave Him the Name that is above every name, that at the name of Jesus every knee should bow, in heaven and on earth and under the earth, and every tongue acknowledge that Jesus Christ is Lord, to the glory of God the Father."*** When Jesus humbled Himself and served, He was exalted. Guess what happens when the husband is exalted? He is esteemed by others, including his wife.

Following the recipe in the right order, will help give you a marriage that is also in order and will flourish! Not only do great leaders serve well, but they do so because they also submit well. Again, 1 Corinthians 11:3 says, ***"But I would have you know, that the Head of every man is Christ; and the head of the woman is the man; and the Head of Christ is God."*** A wife should never lead her husband or "run" her husband. A lot of people think that it's cute, but it is so out of order that the consequences are destruction. Look at Adam and Eve. It was out of order for him to follow what she said when he knew God told him not to touch the Tree of the Knowledge of Good and Evil. A lot of things could've been avoided if Adam led his wife and not her leading him. I want to also make a point in saying that being the head and leading, doesn't mean not submitting to God.

What happens if the man doesn't submit to Christ (follow the recipe)? Well for some men, they run into issues with the wife not submitting. Why? Well it could have a lot to do with the fact that he is sowing rebellion, so in the area of leadership he is reaping rebellion. The husband should never expect a woman to submit to him, if he has not submitted himself to Christ. The problem won't necessarily be that you married a rebellious woman, but sometimes, you married a woman who is great at mimicry. What do I mean? The same way she sees you not respect the authority of Christ, she won't respect yours. Not because you are a bad person, but because you are only getting what you put out. Order flows, but if it gets held up with the husband because he is out of order, he can expect for his household to be out of order as well. As a result, he may lose honor or respect from his wife, so now everything is out of order.

This not only happens with your wife, but if you are a man who doesn't submit to Jesus, then you not only risk your wife not submitting, but also your children as well. Ephesians 6:4 says, ***"And, ye fathers, provoke not your children to wrath: but bring them up in the nurture and admonition of the Lord."*** How can a husband bring his children up in the admonition of the Lord, if he doesn't submit to Jesus? If he's not submitting to Christ, his behavior is not influenced by Christ. Therefore, his actions may provoke his children to wrath. We have to be careful as parents not to provoke our children, because if we provoke them, they have responses that aren't healthy. Colossians 3:21 says, ***"Fathers, provoke not your children to anger, lest they be discouraged."*** A discouraged child will begin to question the desires and visions God has given them and may not be motivated to live purposefully!

God had an excellent example of what a husband who submits will do with his family. Genesis 18:19 says, ***"For I know him, that he will command his children and his household after him, and they shall keep the way of the LORD, to do justice and judgment; that the LORD may bring upon Abraham that which He hath spoken of him."*** Abraham led his family, by submitting to the Lord. Whatever the Lord told Abraham to do, He did. This flowed from him to his wife, and to his son. When Abraham told Sarah the Lord told him to leave his country, Sarah didn't buck against that. She submitted to Abraham's leadership. When Abraham told Isaac that God told him to make a sacrifice and he began to bind him with rope as the sacrifice, nowhere in scripture does it say that Isaac resisted. **Disclaimer: I am not saying anyone should do this to test a child's obedience, but I am using this as an example of Isaac's submission to his father.**

Abraham's entire household replicated his submission to God and they all saw the promises of God as a result. On the contrary, king Saul did not submit to God and things were very chaotic for him. It didn't speak of his wife, but his daughter Michal was contemptuous to her husband David, so God shut up her womb. He lost the respect of his son Jonathan and rightfully so. Then, he and his sons all died on the same battlefield because of his disobedience. Unfortunately, king Saul's lack of submission to God led to destruction for him and his family. This isn't to say that this always happens this way. There are some husbands who are not submitting to God, but may still have a wife who submits to her husband because of her obedience to God and her assignment is in marriage. When I say assignment, I mean that the Word tells the woman to be a help and to submit.

1 Corinthians 7:13-14 says, ***"And the woman which hath an husband that believeth not, and if he be pleased to dwell with her, let her not leave him. For the unbelieving husband is sanctified by the wife, and the unbelieving wife is sanctified by the husband: else were your children unclean; but now are they holy."*** For anyone who understands fulfilling an assignment, they understand the benefits that follow. For the wife, if she is diligent in her assignment of submission, even when the husband is not, she will receive the benefits of her obedience. Lord willing, this may show her husband his submission to God is positioning him to fulfill his assignment as a husband as well.

Now that we understand the order and the role of the husband, we must now understand the role of the wife. We have heard that the wife must submit, but a lot of women take issue with this. However, just as I explain that there is order for the husband as it pertains to service, so is there order for the woman. It also says in Ephesians 5:22, ***"Wives, submit yourselves unto your own husbands, as unto the Lord."*** Most of you new, Webbie inspired women want to be independent so badly! Ok, but never be confused as to why your marriage is not working. Why should you submit, you ask? Ephesians 5:23 says, ***"For the husband is the head of the wife, even as Christ is the Head of the church: and He is the Saviour of the body."*** The wife doesn't submit because her husband demands it, but because there is an order that we must follow.

I won't keep making Eve the bad woman, so I will use Sarah for this example. Before I get on Sarah, I have to say that for the most part, she was very submissive. However, due to Sarah's impatience and possible doubt that her womb would carry the son God promised, she came up with a very emotional idea that caused all kinds of confusion. Abraham was told by God that he and Sarah would have a son, but Sarah decided that Abraham should get her maiden, Hagar, pregnant. Genesis 16:4 says, ***"And he went in unto Hagar, and she conceived: and when she saw that she had conceived, her mistress was despised in her eyes. And Sarai said unto Abram, My wrong be upon thee: I have given my maid into thy bosom; and when she saw that she had conceived, I was despised in her eyes: the LORD judge between me and thee."***

Since she didn't submit to her husband and tried to jump in the leadership position, she brought confusion in her house and it only got worse. Genesis 21:9-10 says, ***"And Sarah saw the son of Hagar the Egyptian, which she had born unto Abraham, mocking. Wherefore she said unto Abraham, Cast out this bondwoman and her son: for the son of this bondwoman shall not be heir with my son, even with Isaac."*** Wives shouldn't feel threatened that the bible tells them to submit. It is not to their detriment, but for their good. Why? God knows that most of us can't handle all the things that can come against a family. Submission doesn't make you any less of a woman, nor does it diminish your position in the Kingdom of God. You and your husband are joint-heirs with Christ and that doesn't change because you submit.

Submission is not so much as obedience to your husband, but it is obedience to God. You're showing God that you want to do what's right, because it pleases Him. Colossians 3:18 NIV says it like this, ***"Wives, submit to your husbands, as is fitting in the Lord."*** It can also be said that if you have a hard time submitting to your husband, that means it would be increasingly difficult for you to submit to God. If you think you can submit to God without submitting to your husband, you're lying to yourself. You're already showing God that you can't submit because you won't submit to His Word to submit to your husband. As I suggested to the wives earlier, I will also say the same thing for the husbands. Some men have wives who don't submit to them, but they remain out of obedience to honor his vows and fulfill his assignment.

1 Corinthians 7:12 says, ***"But to the rest speak I, not the Lord: If any brother hath a wife that believeth not, and she be pleased to dwell with him, let him not put her away."*** If you notice, Paul said these are not words coming from God, but from himself. This could mean that it may not be God's will for us to stay with the unbelieving husband or wife. However, he also says that if they choose to leave, the believing husband or wife is not obligated to stay. 1 Corinthians 7:15-16 says, ***"But if the unbelieving depart, let him depart. A brother or a sister is not under bondage in such cases: but God hath called us to peace. For what knowest thou, O wife, whether thou shalt save thy husband? or how knowest thou, O man, whether thou shalt save thy wife?"*** Paul is saying, don't try to keep what isn't trying to be kept, because you don't know if you will save him or her.

Getting back to the wife, neglecting to submit is bigger than your marriage. This behavior produces an undesirable harvest in your children's behavior towards your husband and you! When you don't submit to your husband, you create an even greater offense for yourself because you're teaching your children this awful behavior. First, it starts with if she is not submitting to her husband, then her children will not submit to their father because they can see that you don't respect his authority. Matthew 18:6 NIV says, ***"If anyone causes one of these little ones—those who believe in me—to stumble, it would be better for them to have a large millstone hung around their neck and to be drowned in the depths of the sea."*** Be mindful of what your disobedience to God (not submitting to your husband) could teach your children.

An unsubmissive wife shouldn't be surprised if she gets that same response out of her children, because she shouldn't expect her children to obey her if she is not following the order of the recipe. Submission to your husband is not only good for your children, but to those who are younger than you who are also watching. Titus 2:3-5 ESV says, ***"Older women likewise are to be reverent in behavior, not slanderers or slaves to much wine. They are to teach what is good, and so train the young women to love their husbands and children, to be self-controlled, pure, working at home, kind, and submissive to their own husbands, that the Word of God may not be reviled."*** Submission is something that older women should teach to younger women because the world is telling them to do something opposite of that. When the older woman is an example to the younger woman. She can then be an example to other young women, but first to her children.

Another reason a wife should submit to her husband as an example to her children, is because when you tell them to honor their mother and father, they see their father being honored by their mother. The example is set. **Sidebar: Both the wife and the husband should set value to their spouse. When children or anyone else is witness to the value and honor you have for your spouse, that's the value and honor they have to treat them with.** Getting back to the children, when they see their mother submit, they will not only respect their father, but they will also follow God's commands because they see her following

God's command to submit to her husband. Parents are some of the most important people in their child's life. Sometimes parents will teach their children through words, and other times through demonstration. Most of the demonstration comes from how you demonstrate to the other parent, your spouse, what you want the child to do.

If it's respect you want the child to give to their parents, it's demonstrated to your spouse. If it is forgiveness you want your child to learn, it's demonstrated to your spouse. Proverbs 22:6 says, ***"Train up a child in the way he should go: and when he is old, he will not depart from it."*** The training is not just what you tell them to do, but what you show them to do. If you don't think a wife's actions have value, look at what a submissive wife can do for her unbelieving husband. 1 Peter 3:1 ESV says, ***"Likewise, wives, be subject to your own husbands, so that even if some do not obey the Word, they may be won without a word by the conduct of their wives, when they see your respectful and pure conduct."*** The question is not what is the Word, but Who is the Word?

John 1:1 tells us the Word, which in the Greek is translated as Logos, is Jesus, who is God. So if the husband is not submitting to Jesus, then the woman beating her husband over the head with the Word is obviously not going to work. Therefore, there needs to be a demonstration of the Word. In the way the wife lives her life, she serves as the example needed for the husband to change. Sometimes wives try to do too much with their words, when the Word of God tells you plainly that the husband is won over by your actions (demonstration of the Word). A man is seldom won over by the wife's words. This is why Proverbs repeats this over and over about the nagging wife:

- Proverbs 19:13 says, ***"A foolish son is his father's ruin, and a quarrelsome wife is like a constant dripping."***
- Proverbs 21:9 says, ***"Better to live on a corner of the roof than share a house with a quarrelsome wife."***
- Proverbs 21:19 says, ***"Better to live in a desert than with a quarrelsome and nagging wife."***
- Proverbs 25:24 says, ***"Better to live on a corner of the roof than share a house with a quarrelsome wife."***
- Proverbs 27:15 says, ***"A quarrelsome wife is like a constant dripping on a rainy day;".***

Proverbs talk about a quarrelsome and nagging wife five times, and twice in the same chapter. Your words, or shall I say nagging, will not make the husband do anything, but leave. Don't believe me, look at each verse! It mentions all the places that are better for a husband to be than around a quarrelsome and nagging wife. The only sad part is that no matter how many times this is mentioned, there are women who will still quarrel with their husbands. This is not to say let a man run all over you! By no means! What it is saying is that you can save your marriage if you stop trying to talk him into doing what you want him to do. Instead live a life that is so exemplary of the Word of God, that it convicts his spirit if he lives contrary to the Word of God.

The problem is not an unbelieving husband or wife not doing what the Word of God says. The problem is a believing husband or wife not demonstrating what the Word of God says to the unbeliever. The catalyst for a husband to change are the actions of the wife, not her words. Her submission to him is evidence that she is obedient to God, because that's what His Word says to do. That type of honor for someone who does not give that honor out or doesn't "deserve it", has to convict a person! If it doesn't, it is definitely motivation! The wife's submission is so critical to the relationships around her, especially that of the one within her household (her husband and children). Her submission is an assignment, not just for her husband, but also for her children.

Not only is it action that wins over her husband, but it is also to teach her children that her honor and submission to her husband is her obedience to God. Therefore, the children's honor to their father and mother is their obedience to God. Your obedience ignites your children's obedience to you and their father, because they will see the Word of God manifested in your life. This is not to take away anything from the father also commanding respect from his children in the example he is to them. I am simply saying that a wife and a mother that lives in obedience to God is a Proverbs 31:28 ESV woman, which says, ***"Her children arise and call her blessed; her husband also, and he praises her:".*** The virtuous woman gets the results of Proverbs 31:28 because a virtuous woman is not a rebellious woman to her husband, but a woman who follows the Word of God.

If both her children and her husband call her blessed and he praises her, that means she is doing right not just as his wife, but as their mother! This is why following the order and recipe of submission is so important in marriage.

Faithful

So the order has been established, the wife submits to the husband, and the husband submits the Christ. Now what? I think it is safe to say that we understand the importance of a wife's submission to her husband, but where a lot of marriages fail is that we don't always understand the husband and wife's submission to each other. This actually helps in the area of fidelity. Ephesians 5:21 ESV says, ***"Submitting to one another out of reverence for Christ."*** We can assume that this particular scripture is for the husband and wife, but we can also assume that it is also for the believer. If we aren't sure if Paul speaks specifically to the husband and wife or to the believer, we can conclude that if he is speaking to the believer and the husband and wife are believers, this is also how they must treat each other.

A good example of submitting to one another is found in 1 Corinthians 7:4-5 NIV, which says, ***"The husband should fulfill his marital duty to his wife, and likewise the wife to her husband. The wife does not have authority over her own body but yields it to her husband. In the same way, the husband does not have authority over his own body but yields it to his wife. Do not deprive each other except perhaps by mutual consent and for a time, so that you may devote yourselves to prayer. Then come together***

again so that Satan will not tempt you because of your lack of self-control." The first thing to take away here is that there is no one-sidedness in marriage. A husband or wife can't say to their spouse you're mine without also saying I'm yours. They also don't say that they are their own. What happens between the two of them is mutual submission and this is what Ephesians 5:21 spoke of as a reverence for God.

In marriage, mutualism is the most beneficial way to operate. Think about it, even if you decided not to have sex, it has to be mutually consented. Fidelity starts with the submission to each other. When you withhold from your spouse, and it's not mutually consented, you are putting them in a position to be tempted. That doesn't mean that some men or women don't have deep rooted issues pertaining to sexual sins that need to be worked out. However, we shouldn't put that person in a situation where it becomes a temptation for them because you're withholding for selfish reasons. If one party decides I am not giving myself to the other, you run into the possibility that satan would try to come in. How? Well, how many of us can fast without food for long periods of time?

For most of us, if we fasted for a few days or so without food and food was continuously brought before us, not many of us would be able to resist eating. Why? Because you're depriving yourself of something your body needs and desires. The same thing with sex, the reason one shouldn't deprive the other for long periods of time, especially when it's not mutually agreed on, is because their possible lack of self control will be used by satan to tempt them. This is not at all to make an excuse for serial cheaters, but even outside of marriage, we are told to not withhold good from those whom it is due. Proverbs 3:27-29 NIV, ***"Do not withhold good from those to whom it is due, when it is in your power to act. Do not say to your neighbor, "Come back tomorrow and I'll give it to you"— when you already have it with you. Do not plot harm against your neighbor, who lives trustfully near you."***

If you have goods that are due to someone and you withhold it, it can cause them to do negative things out of desperation! So if we shouldn't withhold good from others to whom it is due, how much more should you not do it to your spouse when God says that your body belongs to them? God has given us the recipe for fidelity and without that temptation (variable) added, it should give your marriage the desired results.

<u>God is Faithful:</u>

One thing we have to do in all of our relationships is model Christ. Revelation 19:11 NIV says, ***"I saw heaven standing open and there before me was a white horse, whose Rider is called Faithful and True."*** If the husband should love His wife as Christ loves the Church, and Christ is called Faithful, then to be unfaithful is to lie on Christ. Being unfaithful is also not following the recipe, which means you will get undesired results every time. Exodus 34:14 NIV says, ***"Do not worship any other god, for the LORD, Whose name is Jealous, is a jealous God."*** The word worship is a type of intimacy between you and God, so it tells us that God doesn't want His people to be unfaithful to Him by worshiping (showing affection to) other gods. Why? Just like a husband, God is jealous for us. All that means is that He wants what's His and doesn't want to share. When you decide to dishonor your wife by cheating, you show God you can't be trusted with being responsible for what you are asking him for in addition to what you already have.

If God can't trust you with what He gave you, He can't trust you with anything else. Don't believe me? Let's look at Malachi 2:13-14 NIV, ***"Another thing you do: You flood the Lord's altar with tears. You weep and wail because He no longer looks with favor on your offerings or accepts them with pleasure from your hands. You ask, "Why?" It is because the Lord is the witness between you and the wife of your youth. You have been unfaithful to her, though she is your partner, the wife of your marriage covenant."*** Your worship to God or your offerings aren't even favored by God when you have this type of behavior against your wife. This is because every time the husband decides to include the variable of infidelity in the recipe, he will not get the desired results from the recipe of faithfulness.

What Does the Bible Say About the Church?

Before we can give assignments, we must identify who the wife is a representation of in marriage. We can first look at the scripture that gives the husband direction as to how he should operate in his role as the husband. Ephesians 5:25 NIV says, ***"Husbands, love your wives, just as Christ***

loved the church and gave himself up for her." The husband models Christ to love his wife as Christ loves the Church. So here, they compare how the husband should love his wife as Christ loves His Bride, which is the Church. But what does that mean? Ephesians 1:22-23 NIV says, ***"And God placed all things under His feet and appointed Him to be Head over everything for the church, which is His body, the fullness of Him who fills everything in every way."*** In verse 23, it tells us that the Church is Christ's body. This means that the Church, likened to the wife, is Christ Body. This makes so much sense when you think about Ephesians 5:28-30, which says, ***"So ought men to love their wives as their own bodies. He that loveth his wife loveth himself. For no man ever yet hated his own flesh; but nourisheth and cherisheth it, even as the Lord the church: for we are members of His body, of His flesh, and of His bones."***

A husband must love his wife as himself, because she is in fact a part of him. On the other hand, wives must think of themselves as part of their husband. Why? Because man and woman, when they marry, cease to be individuals. At that point they begin to cleave to each other as one flesh. So the wife has to think of herself as the very body of her husband, because this is her origin. Genesis 2:21-24 NIV says, ***"So the Lord God caused the man to fall into a deep sleep; and while he was sleeping, He took one of the man's ribs and then closed up the place with flesh. Then the Lord God made a woman from the rib He had taken out of the man, and He brought her to the man. The man said, "This is now bone of my bones and flesh of my***

flesh; she shall be called 'woman,' for she was taken out of man." That is why a man leaves his father and mother and is united to his wife, and they become one flesh." If the Church is the body of Christ, then the wife is considered the body of her husband. Now how does any of this tell her about her assignment?

Ephesians 5:31 repeats the exact same thing as Genesis 2:24, about, ***"For this reason a man will leave his father and mother and be united to his wife, and the two will become one flesh."*** However, verses 32-33 (NIV) give us some insight to the assignment of the wife. It says, ***"This is a profound mystery—but I am talking about Christ and the church." However, each one of you also must love his wife as he loves himself, and the wife must respect her husband."*** Becoming one flesh is a mystery that describes Christ and His Church. Since we see how the husband should love His wife by looking at how Christ loves the Church, let's look at the Church as the example for how the wife should operate towards her husband in the marriage. Looking at verse 33, the b part tells us that the wife should respect her husband. The Amplified Classic Version says that she should respect and show reverence to him.

One very important thing to start off with is respecting her husband (body). We hear it all the time that women should respect their body and rightfully so. However, isn't it the same thing that scripture is telling wives to do to their husbands? Look at what the Amplified Classic Version says, ***"...and let the wife see that she respects and reverences her husband [that she notices him, regards***

him, honors him, prefers him, venerates, and esteems him; and that she defers to him, praises him, and loves and admires him exceedingly].” Before marriage, if a woman doesn't do this for her own body, there are chances that she may not understand this concept for herself as her husband's body. Go back in this verse and replace him with your, and ask yourself do you have that type of regard for yourself? If not, and you're married, are you struggling in this area? If so, not respecting him or yourself, will cause him to not respect his body, which is you. Make sense? People, especially a man, can tell how you feel about yourself. If he knows you don't have that type of respect for yourself, he won't have that respect for you. If you represent his body, and he doesn't have respect for you, guess what he's disregarding? His own body! I know that's wild, but we have to look at it the way it is.

To get back to the point about fidelity, it is not just expected of the husband, but also of the wife. Exodus 34:14 NIV says, ***“Do not worship any other god, for the Lord, Whose name is Jealous, is a jealous God.”*** As I said earlier, worship was an intimate thing that was exclusive to God. God didn't want His people to worship anyone or anything other than Him, because their marriage required faithfulness to Him. Now let's relate to our marriage. If you are married, you shouldn't be with anyone else in regards to being adulterous! Why would God want to share us with anything or anyone that will defile us or draw us away from Him? God sent His only Son to die on the Cross and instead of our body belonging to Him, we give it to someone else? Why would He want that? Paul said in

2 Corinthians 11:2 ESV says, ***"For I feel a divine jealousy for you, since I betrothed you to one Husband, to present you as a pure virgin to Christ."*** The wife's body must remain pure and true to her husband. Why? Remember, you are your husband's body, so to not respect your body, is to not respect his body as well.

The same way your husband would desire faithfulness of his wife, God desires His body, which is the body of Christ, to be faithful to Him, for His glory. So if either spouse even considered tampering with the recipe and including the variable of infidelity, they will get very undesirable results. We have to have the right perspective about sex. Whatever God created, it was intentional. So, the intentions of sex are not to please our flesh every time we have the urge. The is true for premarital sex as well, but definitely in the confines of marriage. God's intention for sex can be seen for the first time in scripture in the Genesis 1:28, ***"And God blessed them, and God said unto them, Be fruitful, and multiply, and replenish the earth, and subdue it: and have dominion over the fish of the sea, and over the fowl of the air, and over every living thing that moveth upon the earth."***

God created sex as the method that would fulfill His Word to replenish the earth. Sex is one of the most amazing acts of love that God has given to marriage and that act should be exclusive to those two people. Children are the best results of that act. Don't get it twisted! Sex was also for the pleasure and enjoyment of the husband and wife. Again, 1 Corinthians 7:3-5 NIV says, ***"The husband should fulfill***

his marital duty to his wife, and likewise the wife to her husband. The wife does not have authority over her own body but yields it to her husband. In the same way, the husband does not have authority over his own body but yields it to his wife. Do not deprive each other except perhaps by mutual consent and for a time, so that you may devote yourselves to prayer. Then come together again so that Satan will not tempt you because of your lack of self-control." God gives the wife and husband a desire for each other and sex satisfies that desire. It's just like food. Food is used to give the body energy, but God also made it where it was desirable and enjoyable, if used correctly.

Ecclesiastes 9:7 says, ***"Go thy way, eat thy bread with joy, and drink thy wine with a merry heart; for God now accepteth thy works."*** When I say used correctly, I mean that we are not doing things like adding to or taking away anything that would make the food a hindrance to your body. When we abuse food, like overconsumption or eating unhealthy food, it affects the body. Proverbs 23:1-3 says, ***"When thou sittest to eat with a ruler, consider diligently what is before thee: And put a knife to thy throat, if thou be a man given to appetite. Be not desirous of his dainties: for they are deceitful meat."*** Sometimes the problem with food is the same problem married people have with sex, they have an unhealthy appetite for it. Anyone who knows you're married and is offering to give you more of what you already have, is a deceitful tactic of the enemy! Just because it's there or offered to you, don't let your appetite get you in trouble. Proverbs 23:21 says,

"For the drunkard and the glutton shall come to poverty: and drowsiness shall clothe a man with rags."

I'm sure married people having plenty of sex is healthy for them, but wanting to satisfy that desire for sex with someone who is not your spouse is like gluttony. All a gluttonous person is, is someone who misuses and abuses the purpose of food. When you have sex outside of your marriage you are misusing and abusing the purposes of sex. The word for this is called infidelity. The results of infidelity could be in the form of mistrust, trauma, or divorce. I'm not saying that people won't ever get a divorce or that it's not meant for you to get a divorce, but I am saying that usually if both parties are executing this recipe correctly, it's difficult not to succeed. The recipe for fidelity is found in Deuteronomy 7:9, which says, ***"Know therefore that the LORD thy God, He is God, the Faithful God, which keepeth covenant and mercy with them that love Him and keep His commandments to a thousand generations;"***.

God values His covenant so much that He is not only faithful, but He keeps His covenant forever. You should model this in your marriage covenant with your spouse. God had issues with His people being adulterous, because they were gluttonous people. Philippians 3:19 says, ***"Whose end is destruction, whose God is their belly, and whose glory is in their shame, who mind earthly things.)"*** God was all they needed, but they couldn't see that until they experienced undesirable results. The same is for the husband. Proverbs 6:32 says, ***"But whoso committeth***

adultery with a woman lacketh understanding: he that doeth it destroyeth his own soul." You don't want to destroy your marriages, let alone destroy yourself, because if you are destroyed, how can God use you? So adultery could disqualify a person from their purpose if they don't turn from their ways and repent. You have to see marriage a lot deeper than your fleshly appetites. You have to see it for its intended purpose and for what it symbolizes.

I will repeat Ephesians 5:31-33 (NIV) again, which says, ***"For this cause shall a man leave his father and mother, and shall be joined unto his wife, and they two shall be one flesh. This is a great mystery: but I speak concerning Christ and the church. Nevertheless let every one of you in particular so love his wife even as himself; and the wife see that she reverence her husband."*** God has always desired that we be unified with Him. We must not treat marriage like we would if we were dating. To be quite honest, there aren't many examples of people dating around in the Bible, much less dating at all. Marriage isn't a dating show that you can just choose someone else if things didn't work out with you and your spouse. We can't make cheating an option either, just because we want to. It is a symbolism of Christ and the Church. Operating any way contrary to that is to distort the image of Who Christ is to the Church.

Hebrews 13:4 says, ***"Marriage is honourable in all, and the bed undefiled: but whoremongers and adulterers God will judge."*** You honor this symbolism when you are faithful in your marriages. More importantly, we see Christ being that type of Husband to His Church, which we are a member of. You know there are rewards that come from sex with your spouse, when you use it the right way. Physical pleasure and children are just a couple of rewards of sex within the confines of marriage. However, there are also rewards for being faithful. Luke 12:42-44 ESV says, ***"And the Lord said, 'Who then is the faithful and wise manager, whom his master will set over his household, to give them their portion of food at the proper time? Blessed is that servant whom his master will find so doing when he comes. Truly, I say to you, he will set him over all his possessions.'"*** When God can trust you to be faithful with a smaller responsibility, then He gives you more.

Your faithfulness in marriage will cause God to give you more to be faithful over. Marriage is this beautiful symbolism of one of our most important relationships we will ever experience, and that is Christ and the Church. In order for you to get the desired results in your marriage, you must closely model the recipe that Jesus has given you.

Revelation 19:7 says, ***"Let us be glad and rejoice, and give honour to Him: for the marriage of the Lamb is come,***

and His wife hath made herself ready."

You're The Problem, Not...

Parenting/Children

Chapter 11.

I've heard parents say, there aren't any directions to being a parent and I used to think that was correct, but it's not and I will tell you why shortly. Remember when I said at the beginning that my mother taught me how to bake? She gave me the recipe, but before I did it on my own, I saw her do it. Most times when parents teach their children how to bake or anything else, they demonstrate it to them first. I believe God demonstrates to us how to parent by how He Fathers us. John 6:45 says, ***"It is written in the prophets, And they shall be all taught of God. Every man therefore that hath heard, and hath learned of the Father, cometh unto Me."*** Since we are taught by God our Father, we no longer have the excuse, *"There are no directions for parenting"* because we get first-hand instructions on parenting from the Creator of parenthood.

In order for us to have this demonstrated to us properly, the first thing we must embrace is that we are sons and daughters of God. This is important because we don't get the recipe for parenting when we become parents. We get it when we become, and acknowledge we are His sons and daughters. If we pay close attention as His children, we will learn what we need to know about parenting. Psalm 32:8 ESV says, ***"I will instruct you and teach you in the way you should go; I will counsel you with My eye upon you."*** Demonstrating the recipe first is the parent trying to show you the way you should do things. When parents feel like you are ready, it will go from demonstrating the recipe, to allowing you to put into action what you've learned. They are there to counsel you from the sideline and watch to see how you are doing. God taught us as children how to obey Him, so that when we became parents, we would turn around and teach our own children obedience. We teach better when we practice what we teach because we can't teach them anything that we didn't first observe and learn ourselves.

Not only is God teaching us how to be sons and daughters, He is also showing us how to be a parent. Deuteronomy 6:6-7 says, ***"And these words, which I command thee this day, shall be in thine heart: And thou shalt teach them diligently unto thy children, and shalt talk of them when thou sittest in thine house, and when thou walkest by the way, and when thou liest down, and when thou risest up."*** As children of God, if we have paid enough attention to the Father's demonstration, we should be able to teach these same things to our children. When we execute the recipe as parents, we get the desired results in our product, which are our children. As a teacher, I've found that the most productive students are those who know how to follow instructions. The same is true for the Kingdom of God, except, the most productive students are those who know how to follow God's instructions. Ephesians 5:1 says, ***"Be ye therefore followers of God, as dear children;".***

When Paul said this in Ephesians 5:1, he was talking to adults, telling the church to follow God as children, even in their adulthood. Why? Because when you are born again, you may physically be an adult, but spiritually, you are His child, and if you are not spiritually mature, you are still a babe. Hebrews 5:12-14 says, ***"For when for the time ye ought to be teachers, ye have need that one teach you again which be the first principles of the oracles of God; and are become such as have need of milk, and not of strong meat. For every one that useth milk is unskilful in the word of righteousness: for he is a babe. But strong meat belongeth to them that are of full age, even those who by reason of use have their senses exercised to discern both good and evil."*** For most of us, if we have just started following God's instructions or just getting into the Word, we are those babes that He speaks of, even as adults. He is nurturing us as babes, so that we can grow into healthy and mature believers. These healthy believers then turn into healthy parents, because our relationship as children to our Heavenly Father helps us as parents to our children. I believe we can use the Lord's prayer as a model of how we can reconstruct our relationship with God our Father and us with our children. Let's break it down:

"Our Father which art in heaven, hallowed be Thy Name.":

Jesus taught His disciples to pray what many people call the Lord's prayer. I say that because most believe that the Lord's prayer is actually in John 17, when He prayed for His disciples before His crucifixion. Whichever way you've titled the prayer, this was the model prayer that Jesus taught us to pray. It is interesting that it begins with ***"Our Father…"*** because it allows us to see ourselves as His child. This chapter will not help you if you don't see yourself as God's child, because this is what will help the way you see parenting your children. My children don't have the privilege of calling me Ashley. Although that's my name, that is not who I am to them. Someone can ask me the same thing that my children ask me, but because my kids call me mom, I would respond differently.

If we accept God, He is God to us all, but most importantly if we come into relationship with Him, He is our Father. I love that Jesus always called God Father, even though everyone else called Him God. Jesus knew He had certain rights and privileges over everyone else, because He acknowledged Him as Father and not just as God! When we go in prayer saying, *"Our Father…"*, He hears His children and responds to us as our Father. 2 Corinthians 6:17-18 says, ***"Wherefore come out from among them, and be ye separate, saith the Lord, and touch not the unclean thing; and I will receive you. And will be a Father unto you, and ye shall be My sons and daughters, saith the Lord Almighty."*** We have an exclusive relationship with God our Father that separates us from everyone else that hasn't acknowledged Him as their Father. If I were in a room full of people who knew me, I would be Ashley. However, if my children were in that same room, to them I am mommy and I would recognize their voice from everyone else.

God hears the cries of His children the same way a parent can hear their child in a room full of people. When we as children of God call Him Father, we not only separate ourselves from everyone else, but we separate Him from everyone else. When it says, ***"hallowed be Thy Name"***, Bible Study Tools defines hallowed as, *"to make holy or to separate from common."* We set Him above everyone else and everything else. We honor our Father in that way by not making Him like the common things or people around us, because God is more than that. This is how we want to be treated as a parent when our child approaches us about anything. We want them to honor us and set us apart by not treating us in a common way. If we want this respect as parents, we should honor God our Father in that way as well. Exodus 20:12 says, ***"Honour thy father and thy mother: that thy days may be long upon the land which the LORD thy God giveth thee."*** When we honor Him as Father, we access the privilege we have as His children to ask Him what we want that others may not have the privilege to ask that don't acknowledge or honor Him as Father.

<u>Thy Kingdom come, Thy will be done in earth, as it is in heaven:</u>

A lot of times, we struggle with God as His children about relinquishing our will and submitting to the will of the Father. I don't know why we feel like our will is better or the best for our lives, but God knows our every step and He knows what is best for us. Matthew 7:21 says, ***"Not every one that saith unto Me, Lord, Lord, shall enter into the Kingdom of heaven; but he that doeth the will of My Father which is in heaven."*** There are promised results to doing the will of the Father. When we don't do the Father's will, we don't receive the rewards promised to us. Not only that, but if we aren't doing the will of the Father and we begin to see that our children do the opposite of our will, should we really wonder why? We should recognize their disobedience to us as their parents, looks almost exactly, if not exactly like our disobedience to the Father. We must change it in order to get the desired results with our children.

We can take some good pointers from Jesus' relationship with God the Father. The procedures that Jesus followed here on earth were always about the Father's will because He knew what was best for Him and His family (the body of Christ). John 6:38 says, ***"For I came down from heaven, not to do Mine own will, but the will of Him that sent Me."*** Even at the time leading into His crucifixion, Jesus denied what His will was in order to do the will of the Father. When Jesus did the Father's will, His results are found in Matthew 28:18, which says, ***"And Jesus came and spake unto them, saying, All power is given unto Me***

in heaven and in earth." This is a great place where we should really recognize the parallel between God our Father and us as parents and how if we can tell our children how important it is for them to follow our instructions and rules in our home, we have to see the importance of our Heavenly Father's will being done not just in our lives but on the earth.

We should believe that our Father's will is perfect for our lives, just as we try to convince our children that our will is for them. And not so much our will, because I understand that there are some very flawed things happening in parenting styles, but teaching them that the will of our Father being expressed through us is best for them. God not only commands/requires that we obey His will, but He also commands/requires this from our children as well. Colossians 3:20 says, ***"Children, obey your parents in all things: for this is well pleasing unto the Lord."*** It pleases the Lord when our children obey us. It also applies to us as adults who may feel like they no longer have to obey. Our obedience pleases the Lord so much that it deepens our relationship with Him. Matthew 12:50 says, ***"For whosoever shall do the will of My Father which is in heaven, the same is My brother, and sister, and mother."***

God isn't on some power trip with us when He is asking us to do His will, but He wants the very best for us. Not only does it yield amazing results, but it is the right thing to do. Ephesians 6:1 says, ***"Children, obey your parents in the Lord: for this is right."***

"Give us this day our daily bread.":

Matthew 6:31-32 says, ***"Therefore take no thought, saying, What shall we eat? or, What shall we drink? or, Wherewithal shall we be clothed? (For after all these things do the Gentiles seek:) for your heavenly Father knoweth that ye have need of all these things."*** The one thing Jesus tells us not to do as children of God is to worry about our necessities. We may not get all we want, but as His children, God gives us all that we need. God provides for all of creation. Like flowers, some of God's creations don't have a mouth to ask for their needs, yet God provides for them without fail. We are God's children so we don't have to worry about what we need or worry if we will receive it or not. We should also provide this confidence for our children as parents. I understand that there are circumstances that some of us can't help that unfortunately put us in a position to not have everything for our children.

In this case, that's not what I mean. We have to provide our children the confidence that God is not only our Father, but He is also their Father as well! God told David in 1 Chronicles 28:6, ***"And He said unto me, Solomon thy son, he shall build My house and My courts: for I have chosen him to be My son, and I will be His Father."*** God is not just taking care of us and leaving our children to us to figure it out. No, our Father is providing for our children as well! God showed Hagar how faithful He was, not just to her, but also to her child. Genesis 21:17-20 says, ***"And God heard the voice of the lad; and the angel of God called to Hagar out of heaven, and said unto her, What aileth thee, Hagar? fear not; for God hath heard the voice of the lad where he is. Arise, lift up the lad, and hold him in thine***

hand; for I will make him a great nation. And God opened her eyes, and she saw a well of water; and she went, and filled the bottle with water, and gave the lad drink. And God was with the lad; and he grew, and dwelt in the wilderness, and became an archer." One of my former church members named Rhonda, assured a group of mothers at her brunch according to Psalms 127:3, ***"Lo, children are an heritage of the Lord: and the fruit of the womb is His reward."*** She told us that God has our children, because they're His reward (to us).

If God is a Provider for His children, we as parents must also do the same. 2 Corinthians 12:13-14 says, ***"For what is it wherein ye were inferior to other churches, except it be that I myself was not burdensome to you? forgive me this wrong. Behold, the third time I am ready to come to you; and I will not be burdensome to you: for I seek not your's, but you: for the children ought not to lay up for the parents, but the parents for the children."*** This is the case where I am discussing our provision for our children. Our children must never carry the burden, as a child, of providing for us. That is not their place to do that, but our place to do it for them. If you think your children should carry the burden of providing for you or themselves as children, imagine you having to carry for yourself the burden God carries for you. If that is overwhelming for you, don't put that burden on your kids! That's not the recipe!

1 Timothy 5:8 says, ***"But if any provide not for his own, and specially for those of his own house, he hath denied***

the faith, and is worse than an infidel." I am not saying we wouldn't come on hard times. I am saying for parents who may have a mindset that that is the responsibility for the child. That is too heavy of a burden for a child. This is why when we are constantly trying to help God by doing things to make things happen, it always feels burdensome to us. That's because God never intended for us to carry our own burdens, nor did He ever intend for us to do things to "help" Him with our situation. God doesn't need our help. He is an amazing Provider! 1 Peter 5:7 says, ***"casting all your cares upon Him, for He careth for you."*** If there is a need we have in taking care of children, the burden shouldn't be cast on the child, but on God! He is the One Who will help us to provide for everyone and everything we are responsible for.

We need to learn to rest in His provision and allow God to lift the burden and provide. How we receive God is also how we are teaching our children to receive God. Therefore, we must teach our children to do this so that when they are older, they don't make the mistake of trying to carry burdens that aren't theirs, or worse, casting their burdens on their kids!

<u>And forgive us our debts, as we forgive our debtors.:</u>

God is such a forgiving Father. We fall short so many times, but just like a loving Father, He forgives us. So guess what? We also must forgive our children. Psalms 103:12-13, ***"As far as the east is from the west, so far hath He removed our transgressions from us. Like as a father pitieth his children, so the LORD pitieth them that fear***

Him." The one thing that we have to understand is that God doesn't hold a grudge. He corrects and forgives us, then He removes the transgression from us so that He can't keep looking at it. God isn't bringing it back up and He isn't continuing to punish us for something He has already forgiven us for. One incredible act of forgiveness is found in Luke 15:21-23, which says, ***"And the son said unto him, father, I have sinned against heaven, and in thy sight, and am no more worthy to be called thy son. But the father said to his servants, Bring forth the best robe, and put it on him; and put a ring on his hand, and shoes on his feet: And bring hither the fatted calf, and kill it; and let us eat, and be merry:"***.

We have to let our children know that we are forgiving them, not because we are these amazing parents, but because we are forgiving them to show them how amazing God our Father is to ALWAYS forgive us! This is the one thing about parenting that I think a lot of us miss the mark on. We sometimes neglect to consider how God has forgiven us. Therefore, it causes us to judge our children to an extent that God, Our Father, has not judged us. Think about it. It's called forGIVEness, which means God gave it to us so that we have it in our possession to GIVE to others. If we choose not to give our children what we know we have (forgiveness), we are lying on God and ultimately saying that we don't have it (forgiveness) to give. Jesus told a parable of an evil servant who begged for mercy from his master, yet turned around and wasn't merciful to the servant under him.

When his master found out, he said in Matthew 18:32-33, ***"Then the master called the servant in. 'You wicked servant,' he said, 'I canceled all that debt of yours because you begged me to. Shouldn't you have had mercy on your fellow servant just as I had on you?'"*** The master was upset because he knew he gave the servant forgiveness so that meant he possessed forgiveness, to give to the other servant. So what do we think God's response will be when we refuse to show mercy on others? Matthew 18:34-35 says, ***"In anger his master handed him over to the jailers to be tortured, until he should pay back all he owed. "This is how My heavenly Father will treat each of you unless you forgive your brother or sister from your heart."*** The torture may not always be physical, but can be just as much mental and emotional because you can be treated by God the same way you treat others. Understand that once we receive anything from God, like forgiveness, we don't just receive it for ourselves.

We also receive forgiveness so that we can give to others. Whenever we don't have mercy on someone else, especially our children, we are saying, *"I don't have it to give to you"* or better yet, *"God didn't give it to me, so I don't have it to give."* This is the biggest lie we tell on God! It wouldn't be bad if He didn't give it to us, because God wouldn't expect us to give anything we don't have. Just like forgiveness, we know that we all have mercy to give because Psalms 23:6 tells us ***"Surely goodness and mercy shall follow me all the days of my life"***. Can you imagine why goodness and mercy follows us all the days of our life? It's probably because God wanted to make sure we had enough to give to those around us. Therefore, we should forgive our children as we are forgiven by our heavenly Father. I have to be honest; I sometimes get annoyed when I feel like I am being led to be compassionate with something that I know one of my children did wrong. In that moment, I may or may not want to be compassionate, but when I begin to think of my shortcomings I am reminded of the compassion God showed me.

I try to think of every excuse as to how it's not the same, but somehow, it ends up being revealed to me that it's my mirror experience. Lamentations 3:22-23 NIV says, ***"Because of the Lord's great love we are not consumed, for His compassions never fail. They are new every morning;* great *is your faithfulness."*** All glory to God! As much as I want to drive home a point with my kids, I realize I got up that morning praying that God would be compassionate towards me. This realization helps me to understand that as much as God is compassionate towards me as His daughter, I should be the same way with my children. Why? Because compassion is a part of the recipe for parenting! God's compassion towards us is related to a father's compassion towards his children. Psalm 103:13 says, ***"As a father shows compassion to his children, so the Lord shows compassion to those who fear Him."***

I am sometimes moved with emotions when I explain to my kids why I am forgiving them. I ask them, *"Do you know why I am forgiving you?"* They will respond from what I told them prior, *"Because God forgives you?"* This is the time where I am showing them what God gives to me as my Father, I also give them as my children. Why? Because I have it to give. As a matter of fact, God giving me forgiveness could be more about my children than it is about me. Hopefully, it shows them how to operate with others as well. All glory to God! I don't want my children to feel like I don't understand what they are going through. Neither does Jesus want us to feel like He doesn't understand what we are going through. Hebrews 4:15 says, ***"For we do not have a High Priest Who is unable to sympathize with our weaknesses, but we have One Who was tempted in every way that we are, yet was without sin."***

Jesus knew how we felt and although He didn't sin, He knew it was a hard thing to try to overcome certain things. So, I try to show them that as much as they are learning and having to follow instructions, I am too. And just like them, I fall short. This is why I get a little emotional when I realize the Father's compassion towards me and it happens when I am put in a position to show compassion to my kids.

"And lead us not into temptation, but deliver us from evil:"

I know most of us are thinking that we wouldn't lead our children into temptation. However, there are ways that we actually can and we have to be careful not to do it. Ephesians 6:4 says, ***"Fathers, do not provoke your children to anger, but bring them up in the discipline and instruction of the Lord."*** Sometimes we can do things that cause our children to have a response that doesn't align with what God says about them. If we are rude, mean, or sarcastic to our children, this may turn them from their innocence and negatively impact how they respond to you or to others. You provoking your child is the unnecessary actions that you take in raising them that could potentially harden them. God does not chasten us to the point of anger or push us to the point where we want to give up. Psalms 103:8-10 says, ***"The Lord is merciful and gracious, slow to anger, and plenteous in mercy. He will not always chide: neither will He keep His anger for ever. He hath not dealt with us after our sins; nor rewarded us according to our iniquities."***

The way God handles us doesn't provoke us, because He knows it will discourage us. We should look at this step in the recipe and follow God's lead with our children. Colossians 3:21 says, ***"Fathers, do not provoke your children, lest they become discouraged."*** This is why we have to be mindful in the way that we correct our children. God always seems to use my children (and occasionally other people) to show me things about myself that I didn't know were there! This happened to David when he slept with Bathsheba and had her husband put on the front line to be killed, because he got her pregnant. Afterwards, the prophet Nathan told him a story of a rich man and a poor man. The poor man only had one lamb that he loved dearly and he said in 2 Samuel 12:4, ***"Now a traveler came to the rich man, but the rich man refrained from taking one of his own sheep or cattle to prepare a meal for the traveler who had come to him. Instead, he took the ewe lamb that***

belonged to the poor man and prepared it for the one who had come to him."

David was so upset with the rich man that he said the man should be killed for doing that. In most cases this would be justice, except the prophet Nathan revealed to David in 2 Samuel 12:7, ***"You are the man!".*** David didn't realize that the judgment he gave the man was actually judgment against himself. Guess what? This is us as parents. We see our children behaving a certain way and we are ready to throw down. However, may I suggest to you that perhaps their behavior towards you mirrors your behavior towards your heavenly Father so that you may see yourself. Is it possible that with the same judgment you pass, you may be warned that you are subject to the same judgment being passed upon you? It also may be God's way of allowing you to see the same way you feel your child's behavior should be corrected, is your suggestion to the Father of the best way to correct your behavior.

I know, this is tough to swallow, but you have to admit that there is some, if not total truth to it. I am not saying we shouldn't discipline our children. I am simply saying that in disciplining them, our discipline should hopefully cause them to self reflect and help steer them in the right direction. It is the same way God's correction encourages us. If we took heed to what God is trying to correct in our lives, the same way we want our children to, maybe we could avoid the consequences. In David's case, he definitely received the punishment he decided was appropriate for the rich man, but in a different way.

Unfortunately, he lost the son that was conceived from his sin. However, God, in His love, blessed David with a son that would one day build God's temple! Again, God's correction or the way He handles us doesn't and shouldn't discourage us. It should help us to make better decisions and, in essence, make us become better individuals. If what you are doing to correct your child is causing a negative response, you may need to pray for guidance, because you could be doing something that is provoking them and ultimately discouraging them.

If you are unsure if what you are doing with your child is productive or counterproductive, a good rule of thumb is to look at how God handles you and use that as a model.

For Thine is the Kingdom, and the power, and the glory, for ever. Amen.:

I have to be honest again. I had to look this part of Matthew 6:13 up in different translations because I really wanted to make sure I had the correct revelation. You cannot fully understand this part of the verse if you don't know what precedes it. The "A" part of Matthew 6:13 says, ***"And lead us not into temptation, but deliver us from evil:"*** This part of the verse is asking something of someOne Who is perceived to be the One Who has the power to do it. I guess the question that should follow is, *"Why that Person?"* The reason anyone could ask anything of anyone is if they knew that person had the ability or power to do it. In my humble opinion, that's what the "B" part of Matthew 6:13 says. We can ask the Father to lead us not into temptation and deliver us from evil, because the Kingdom, Power, and Glory, are

His Forever… I know for some this is a rather bold statement, but if you believe it, you say, "Amen" to these things, because "Amen" means, "so be it!"

When scripture says, ***"Thine is the Kingdom…"***, this means that the Kingdom belongs to God. Psalms 24:1 confirms this when it says, ***"The earth is the LORD's, and the fulness thereof; the world, and they that dwell therein."*** If God is our Father and the earth is the LORD's then what does that say about us? I've heard Dr. Myles Munroe say that God has given us kingdoms in the earth that we have dominion over. One of those kingdoms that God has given us dominion over, has to be our home. Therefore, as it pertains to our kingdom (home), we determine what can and can't happen within those four walls. Whether evil or temptations try to come against us or our children, our heavenly Father has given us authority to keep temptation and evil from us and our families.

We just learned that when scripture says, ***"Thine is the Kingdom"***, that means our Father is the King of that domain. Therefore, if we are modeling our parenting after the Father, the kingdom, in this case, is our home. We must first give Him dominion and rule in our home. When we do that, He makes us kings and queens of our homes, So what about when it says, ***"Thine is… the power…"***? It is saying that, because He has power, we become vessels of that power in our kingdom (home). That means He gives us power and ability. 1 Corinthians 4:20 says, ***"For the Kingdom of God is not in word, but in power."*** God doesn't have to talk about what He can do, because He has the ability to do whatever you ask of Him. So if we ask God to keep us from evil and lead us not into temptation, guess what, He has the ability to do it! 1 Corinthians 10:13 says, ***"There hath no temptation taken you but such as is common to man: but God is faithful, Who will not suffer you to be tempted above that ye are able; but will with the temptation also make a way to escape, that ye may be able to bear it."***

God will always give us a way to get out of any temptation because he has the power to do that! As His sons and daughters, God has also given us the ability to do whatever it is that He has called us to do in the earth, especially as it pertains to our children. **2 Peter 1:3 says, *"According as His divine power hath given unto us all things that pertain unto life and godliness, through the knowledge of Him that hath called us to glory and virtue:"*.** When we recognize that God, through His divine power and ability, has given us everything that we need for life, and godliness has not only given us what we need for life, but also given us what we need to be a parent. The very things that have to be done, we are able to do, through His power. Moreover, the same way He keeps us, He keeps our children through us. We have the ability to keep our children from evil and temptations that try to present themselves to them.

We aren't depending on ourselves, but on our heavenly Father. Romans 11:36 says, ***"For of Him, and through Him, and to Him, are all things: to Whom be glory for ever. Amen."*** Everything is to the glory of God. Why? Because the Kingdom and the Power are all His. We aren't the ones keeping our children. God is keeping our children, through us! That's why it is to His glory! And since God is living in us, His glory is reflected through us. Psalms 3:3 says, ***"But Thou, O Lord, art a Shield for me; my Glory, and the Lifter Up of mine head."*** We aren't reflecting God's glory for ourselves, but to glorify Him. When we pray for our children and command our homes to be a house of prayer, the protection our children experience may seem like it's our glory, but we do it to redirect that glory back to God! 1 Corinthians 10:31 says, ***"Whether therefore ye eat, or drink, or whatsoever ye do, do all to the glory of God."***

Whatever we do, it should bring God glory, Why? Because the glory belongs to Him. Our possession of our kingdom and the power and ability He gives us with His power, begins with acknowledging that the Source of it all is from God. 1 Chronicles 29:11, which says, ***"Thine, O LORD, is the greatness, and the power, and the glory, and the victory, and the majesty: for all that is in the heaven and in the earth is Thine; Thine is the Kingdom, O LORD, and Thou art exalted as head above all."*** Since we are the image of the Father, our confidence is that the dominion and the ability to do for our children is from God and to the glory of God!

Despise Not the Chastening:

As our heavenly Father, He knows we won't get it right every time, but He corrects us and helps us get back on track. Proverbs 3:11-12, ***"My son, despise not the chastening of the LORD; neither be weary of His***

correction: For whom the LORD loveth He correcteth; even as a father the son in whom he delighteth." I love that it says ***"... the LORD loveth He correcteth…"***, meaning, He loves those He corrects. To be corrected isn't as bad as it feels. It hurts sometimes to be corrected, but correction helps us to not miss the mark in that area again. As parents, we understand the love aspect when we discipline our children, but we don't always understand the love aspect of God's discipline to us, as His children. If we don't see love in God's discipline, it affects how we handle discipline issues with our own children.

If I can be completely honest (again), there have been times I didn't discipline my kids, because I didn't want God to discipline me in that same area. For some reason, I group this in the same category of when I am showing my kids compassion. However, it is not the same. As compassionate as this may seem, this is not compassion, it's selfishness. Proverbs 13:24 says, ***"He that spareth his rod hateth his son: but he that loveth him chasteneth him betimes."*** God teaches me how to love my children in the way He loves me. He doesn't just love me when He gives me awesome gifts. He also demonstrates His love for me when He chastens me to correct behavior that will hinder me. It's selfish if I don't discipline my children, because I don't want it in return from God! Even though I don't want God to chasten me, that doesn't mean I shouldn't discipline or chasten my children, because it's not love to withhold chastening. It actually calls it hate! Whew!

God's love is demonstrated to me by correction because it teaches me boundaries. When I refuse to do that with my children, I am doing both me and my children a disservice! This is not to say that because I fall short that I never discipline my children. I still have to correct them, because I understand that, although I am still learning as a child of God, I am still a parent who has been entrusted with my children. One part of parenting that we have been entrusted to do is to correct, because that is the part that helps to develop character and, in essence, saves them. Proverbs 23:13-14 ESV says, ***"Do not withhold discipline from a child; if you strike him with a rod, he will not die. If you strike him with the rod, you will save his soul from Sheol."*** If we understand that disciplining our children saves them, then why do we not understand this principle as children of God when it comes to us being disciplined?

What if your child is not rebellious, but their behavior is God using it as a mirror to reflect back to you your rebellion to Him? The reason I say that is because I've noticed that my children have things about them that I absolutely love that remind me of me! However, there are things I see in them that I also see in myself that need correction. Doesn't that sound very similar to a mirror?

Parents and Children Are Schoolmates:

It is almost like us and our children are in school together. This is not to be confused that we are on the same level, but that we are all still learning and will continue to learn as we get older. Although my brother and I were both students, he was in high school and I was in elementary school. This means we were on different levels. Although parents and their children aren't on the same level, we are all still learning together. When God gave us our children, He let us know right then that He trusts us to be parents. What's interesting is that while we are parents, we are still learning as children of God. At the same time, we are leading our children, even though we may still fall short being children of God. Therefore, we must not blame the child for following the disobedience/rebellion they see in us. Rather, we should set the example as disciplined children to our Father, so they in turn will know how to be disciplined children to us.

Hebrews 12:7-11 tells us how to respond to discipline. Beginning with verse 7 (NIV), it says, ***"Endure hardship as discipline; God is treating you as His children. For what children are not disciplined by their father?"*** I only discipline my kids so that they will know not to do or to do certain things. I never want my kids to feel like what I am doing is only to hurt them, because it's not true. The sting from discipline is teaching them that wrong choices hurt and you avoid future hurt if you learn from that lesson. However, if you keep doing it, you keep feeling the sting of discipline. Unfortunately, that sting is not always the same as it was initially and can get more and more intense if you don't learn your lesson the first time. Furthermore, verse 8 tells us the other truth about discipline, ***"If you are not disciplined—and everyone undergoes discipline—then***

you are not legitimate, not true sons and daughters at all."

If I see a child that's not mine doing something wrong, I'm not going to discipline them, because they are not my child to discipline. I only discipline my children. If you're not disciplined by God or reject His correction, you're saying to God, *"I am not Your child, so You don't have that authority/right to discipline me."* Usually if a child goes undisciplined, it doesn't turn out well. Proverbs 29:15 says, ***"A rod and a reprimand impart wisdom, but a child left undisciplined disgraces its mother."*** As much as being disciplined sucks, we shouldn't allow our children to go undisciplined. If our children were going around cutting up and telling people they're our children, we would be so embarrassed because their actions don't display the way we're raising them! However, we walk around telling people we are children of God but don't realize we embarrass God because we are so undisciplined.

Not literally embarrass God, but we make being His child look so reckless sometimes! If our children did what we do, we would want to check it right there. Hebrews 12:9-10 reminds us that, ***"Moreover, we have all had human fathers who disciplined us and we respected them for it. How much more should we submit to the Father of spirits and live! They disciplined us for a little while as they thought best; but God disciplines us for our good, in order that we may share in His holiness."*** What if when we received correction, we wouldn't take it as a punishment, but as tough love that helps develop our character? I don't even know if I will say it's tough love, but it's love. I can remember being younger and my peers and I would joke on what some of our parents would say when we were getting disciplined. They would say things like, *"I'm doing this because I love you."* For me, that was the dumbest thing I heard, but that was because I didn't understand what love would do to keep you from living a foolish life! I felt like if they loved me, they wouldn't want to discipline me, but that's why corrections can get complicated if we don't have love.

Proverbs 13:24 says, ***"Whoever spares the rod hates his son, but he who loves him is diligent to discipline him."*** Love is correction that costs a little sting now, before you learn a more painful lesson that costs a lot more hurt later. If you endure it, it produces the right behavior. I notice that every time I don't do this with my children, it gets harder to correct the next time. Therefore, I am doing more harm than good by not chastening them! The same is to be said about parents. Love would rather discipline you for that moment instead letting life hurt you for a lifetime. Anyone who knows the consequences of bad behavior and over looks it means they are letting you set yourself up for a lifetime of hurt, and to me, that's not love. Only someone who hates you or secretly wants to see you in a bad situation wouldn't step in and tell you better or discipline you!

If we are not disciplining our children, but wondering why we are getting the wrong results, we don't have to look any further than the fact that we aren't following the recipe. Hebrews 12:11 says, ***"Now no chastening for the present***

seemeth to be joyous, but grievous: nevertheless afterward it yieldeth the peaceable fruit of righteousness unto them which are exercised thereby." If we're ok as parents disciplining our children, because we know it's for their good, we should also accept that God disciplines us for our good. God will give you discernment when to share this (I advise being led by the Holy Spirit), but I honestly think that when we are chastened by God, sometimes the "why" behind you being disciplined shouldn't be hidden from our children, because they should see that you don't stop getting disciplined when you do wrong. Or rather, you shouldn't think that aging diminishes your discipline because it doesn't.

It's good for our children to know that they shouldn't have the mindset that *"When I'm older, I will do whatever I want,"* because it's an unrealistic expectation that will end with disappointment. As I said earlier, we are all still learning and will continue to learn as long as we are alive! Sometimes, after my oldest daughter has been corrected for something, I have shared with her that I am in or have been in a situation similar to hers where I am or was being disciplined as a child of God. That moment lets her know that she's not alone and as a result, she doesn't feel overwhelmed with missing the mark. Romans 3:23 tells us that, ***"for all have sinned and fall short of the glory of God,".*** I let her know I understand how she feels, because I also get disciplined when I fall short. I tell her that I don't always like how it feels either to be disciplined, but I know that it is for our good.

The NIV translation of Hebrews 12:11 says, ***"No discipline seems pleasant at the time, but painful. Later on, however, it produces a harvest of righteousness and peace for those who have been trained by it."*** Even as I write, I am reminded that although I don't like discipline, just like I would want my children to understand, I understand that it's ultimately for our good. I want to make sure that we don't get disciplining confused with being a puppeteer. God isn't giving parents the liberty to correct behavior by dictation or abuse. Nor does God want to or wants us to discipline from a place of anger or frustration. Psalms 38:1 says, ***"O Lord, rebuke me not in Thy wrath: neither chasten me in Thy hot displeasure."*** If my example is God, I wouldn't want Him to call "discipline" love, but He is doing it from a place of anger! I know that if He did that, it would push me in the opposite direction.

If God doesn't do us like that, then we shouldn't do our children like that either! Let's look at Ephesians 6:4 again, but from the amplified version. It says, ***"Fathers, do not provoke your children to anger [do not exasperate them to the point of resentment with demands that are trivial or unreasonable or humiliating or abusive; nor by showing favoritism or indifference to any of them], but bring them up [tenderly, with lovingkindness] in the discipline and instruction of the Lord."*** Love is associated with discipline because when the discipline is from a place of love, it shapes and molds their character. If it's done from a place of anger or frustration, it tears down and breaks character. Our love in discipline is simply saying that we shouldn't allow bad behavior to go uncorrected, because if it gets too out of hand, it could negatively affect the future and be hard to control. Going past correction because we are angry or just for the sake of being a parent is provoking them to anger and can create a monster you won't be able to control in the future. It's also to discipline the lives we live as well.

What would happen if we lived a more disciplined life? We would be better examples of what we want from our children by demonstrating self-control, so that when we ask them to be self-controlled, they mirror our example. Paul said to the church at Philippi, in Philippians 4:9, ***"Those things, which ye have both learned, and received, and heard, and seen in me, do: and the God of peace shall be with you."*** He knew that in order for him to have the results in those who followed him, he had to first be a great example. I was telling my sister that I can't tell my children that it's unhealthy to eat treats every night, but they see that I still eat them every night. I told her I had to be the example of what I was asking them to do, otherwise, I would look like a hypocrite! Paul understood this as a leader.

If Paul asked his fellow coworkers of the faith or the churches he visited to do anything, he knew he had to demonstrate it first. For instance, if he wanted them to discipline their bodies, he had to do it first. Why? In 1 Corinthians 9:27, he says, ***"No, I strike a blow to my body and make it my slave so that after I have preached to others, I myself will not be disqualified for the prize."*** He is essentially saying that the discipline he preaches to others, he himself continues to practice, or rather, initiates, so he won't miss out on the reward God promises for it. I remember the Holy Spirit checking me about what I was telling one of my children about something they should improve on. When He reminded me, I had to first admit to myself in that moment that I also fell short with God in that area too. I then told my child that this was also an area that I fell short in and that we were both going to work on it together. Schoolmates, remember? It actually helped me to try to work on it, because I knew from that point on my kids would be watching to see if I was actually going to do better like I said.

This was a form of accountability for me because I knew that I had something or someone to remind me to practice what I preached. Think about it, I am not leading my kids off of what I say, but what the Word of God says. So, if I tell my child that they should do something, and I don't do it, they can walk away thinking, *"If it's the right thing to do, why is she not doing it too?"* Romans 2:19-24 NIV says, ***"if you are convinced that you are a guide for the blind, a light for those who are in the dark, an instructor of the foolish, a teacher of little children, because you have in the law the embodiment of knowledge and truth—you, then, who teach others, do you not teach yourself? You who preach against stealing, do you steal? You who say that people should not commit adultery, do you commit adultery? You who abhor idols, do you rob temples? You who boast in the law, do you dishonor God by breaking the law? As it is written: "God's name is blasphemed among the Gentiles because of you."***

Having the knowledge of the truth and not living it is what causes people (especially unbelievers) to call believers hypocrites. What is worse than that are children of believers who see their parents not practice what they preach, and they are seen as hypocrites, or cause them to grow up doing the same thing! I couldn't tell my kids that I believed in something so passionately, yet I didn't apply those same principles to my life. Better yet, if I don't show that those principles have value in my personal life, it would make the things of God and His Word look like a joke. If the Word is such a guide, why aren't we letting it guide our lives? They grow up thinking that the Word of God is just rules for children, and when you get older, you have the liberty to do them or not. Or worse, they think when they get older, the Word doesn't apply to them and holds no value in their lives.

We will be quick to call a young adult a backslider for this, but some are simply following your lead. Maybe some bad habits or ways of thinking are developed in our children because we pass on the wrong recipe to them. I am not saying that parents are always the reason their children may become disobedient or rebellious. That is definitely not the point I am trying to make! I am only suggesting that if you're only preaching and not practicing the Word of God, you're communicating to your children your true estimation of the value that the Word of God has in your own life, let alone theirs. This is why in that moment of correcting my child, I had a decision to make. Either I wasn't going to hold my children to certain expectations because I wasn't willing to correct my own behavior, or I was going to discipline myself and lead by example. I had to and still have to make the decision that I am not going to lower the bar for my children just because I don't want to rise up to the standard as well.

I have to keep the standard and hold myself accountable in the areas I want my child to do better in. This doesn't mean that when we have times that we slip up, we shouldn't correct our child. Correction is still in order, but you may have to humble yourself and work on that area too, so that you can be the example of the standard you are holding them to. We don't want to just lead our children in what we tell them to do, but show them as well. We also don't just lead by what we say, but in what Christ did. Jesus remains the standard and our leading should be as Paul told the church in 1 Corinthians 11:1, ***"Be ye followers of me, even as I also am of Christ."*** I am not the standard, Christ is. Therefore, the way I lead my children is not based on what I would do, but how Christ told me to do it in His Word.

I think most parents feel like if their children hear them admit that they fall short, they will look at them differently. Honestly, you may be running the risk of it. However, my job as a parent is to be an example and where I fall short and get up and try to do better, is also an example of growth, maturity, and taking accountability. Our children have to know that they will fall short, but they also have to know that they can get up from there. Proverbs 24:16 says, ***"For a just man falleth seven times, and riseth up again: but the wicked shall fall into mischief."*** Why is this important for them to know? Because they will have challenges in their life and if they think that there is no grace for the times they miss the mark, they will give up on trying to grow in that area.

I am not saying that our children need to be privy to all of our shortcomings. An example of this is when one of Noah's sons saw his father's nakedness and exposed him to his brothers and was cursed as a result of it. I understand that some things aren't for them to see or know, because they may not be mature enough to handle it. However, there are going to be times, the Holy Spirit will lead you to allow them to witness it. It's not so much about them seeing us fall as it is them seeing how we respond to it. This is another opportunity for them to see God's grace to continue to pursue what is right. I would rather them see me humble myself and make the proper corrections, than to make excuses for my wrong behavior, due to pride.

Pride may help you look good for the moment, but it won't help you avoid destruction. Proverbs 16:18 says, ***"Pride goeth before destruction, and an haughty spirit before a fall."*** Your pride could be detrimental to both you and your child. For you, because you're in pride and that leads down a destructive path. For the child, because it teaches them behavior(s) that could lead them down a destructive path as well. It may help us as parents if we remove the thought that this is more about parenting than it is about being a child of God. I was a child of God before I was a parent, so I am obligated to live a life that is pleasing to Him, first! If I begin to live my life as a child of God rather than just as a parent, my focus wouldn't be on how my child sees my flaws or will look at me differently. Instead, the focus will be on how, as a child of God, He sees me differently, even when I fall short. The differently that God sees us is in His image. Isaiah 62:2-3 says, ***"And the Gentiles shall see thy righteousness, and all kings thy glory: and thou shalt be called by a new name, which the mouth of the LORD shall name. Thou shalt also be a crown of glory in the hand of the LORD, and a royal diadem in the hand of thy God."***

For me personally, when I was willing to humble myself and do the work, I went from the parent of my child, to the child of God (our heavenly Father). I allowed God to teach me what I needed to do from that point on. This helped me focus my attention on doing better as God's child, and as a result, I present a better example for my children as their parent. Proverbs 20:7 says, ***"The just man walketh in his integrity: his children are blessed after him."*** The area I did better in, I could expect and know that my child could have the same experience with correction and do better in that area also. Why? Because the recipe promises those results and I am the product of that recipe that proves those results.

<u>But, why?:</u>

When each of my kids got to the inquisitive age, one of the questions they would ask when I would tell them to do or not to do something would be, *"Why?"* Although being aware of the why is important, not all the time will what you say make sense to your child, the same way what God tells you doesn't always make sense to you. When it doesn't make sense, they're going to want to know why. The things we feel they should know, we tell them. However, there are times when we aren't going to give our children the *"why"* because, in certain situations, it isn't for them to know. Deuteronomy 29:29 says, ***"The secret things belong unto the LORD our God: but those things which are revealed belong unto us and to our children for ever, that we may do all the words of this law."*** Whether we realize it or not, there are things that we just can't handle knowing right now. Just like parents with their children, there are times that God may not always reveal to us why.

Abraham was asked a hard thing from God and he didn't disclose to Isaac what he was going to do. Genesis 22:7-8 says, ***"And Isaac spake unto Abraham his father, and said, My father: and he said, Here am I, my son. And he said, Behold the fire and the wood: but where is the lamb for a burnt offering? And Abraham said, My son, God will provide Himself a lamb for a burnt offering: so they went both of them together."*** As a parent, there are times that I have a reason why I don't share everything with my children. There are times they may not understand or may be too young and God knows the same thing about us. Acts 1:7 says, ***"And He said unto them, It is not for you to know the times or the seasons, which the Father hath put in His own power."*** Isaac had to obey Abraham when I know it made no sense to him to do so.

Genesis 22:9-13 says, ***"And they came to the place which God had told him of; and Abraham built an altar there, and laid the wood in order, and bound Isaac his son, and***

laid him on the altar upon the wood. And Abraham stretched forth his hand, and took the knife to slay his son. And the Angel of the LORD called unto him out of heaven, and said, Abraham, Abraham: and he said, Here am I. And He said, Lay not thine hand upon the lad, neither do thou any thing unto him: for now I know that thou fearest God, seeing thou hast not withheld thy son, thine only son from Me. And Abraham lifted up his eyes, and looked, and behold behind him a ram caught in a thicket by his horns: and Abraham went and took the ram, and offered him up for a burnt offering in the stead of his son." Even though Isaac didn't know why, there is nowhere in the bible that said that he resisted his dad's command to lay down and be strapped down in the place of the sacrifice.

Abraham probably didn't tell Isaac that he was going to be the sacrifice because he may have known that it was too much for Isaac to handle and that he may not have even cooperated. (This also could've affected Abraham's emotions and if he would've continued to go through with it). Imagine if Isaac wasn't cooperative because he didn't know the "why". Neither he nor Abraham would've seen God's salvation and provision. God knows that if I knew when Jesus was coming back, when the rapture was, or when it was my time to transition, I would most certainly live life differently. So, we have to trust that He knows that if we knew everything, it would affect how we respond to everything else, including Him. God doesn't even share Jesus' return with the angels just to make sure no one tries to leak this information to you too soon. Matthew 24:36

says, ***"But of that day and hour knoweth no man, no, not the angels of heaven, but My Father only."*** Although our children don't know why, we as parents still expect them to do what we ask them to do. We must understand that as a child of God, even if it doesn't make sense, it doesn't mean we have to wait until it does in order for us to obey God.

Some things aren't for us to know in order for us to trust God. Sometimes, we just have to trust Him without knowing why, because God knows that in some cases, ignorance is bliss. On the other hand, children aren't always being disrespectful when they ask why. They just want to understand. God understood this and said in Deuteronomy 6:20-25, ***"In the future, when your son asks you, "What is the meaning of the stipulations, decrees and laws the Lord our God has commanded you?" tell him: "We were slaves of Pharaoh in Egypt, but the Lord brought us out of Egypt with a mighty hand. Before our eyes the Lord sent signs and wonders—great and terrible—on Egypt and Pharaoh and his whole household. But He brought us out from there to bring us in and give us the land He promised on oath to our ancestors. The Lord commanded us to obey all these decrees and to fear the Lord our God, so that we might always prosper and be kept alive, as is the case today. And if we are careful to obey all this law before the Lord our God, as He has commanded us, that will be our righteousness."***

Sometimes it gets annoying when our children ask why, because it seems like they don't trust us. However, God doesn't get annoyed with us when we want to know why. When God told the Israelites to tell their children the things that happened to them, it was strategic. God knew that once their children understood not only why they obeyed God's decrees and laws, but also that by their obedience, when they grew up, they would do and teach their children to do the same thing. God knows the importance of children understanding why they are doing something. It teaches them to understand cause and effect, as well as the rewards of obedience and the consequences of disobedience. The motivation that every child needs to obey is knowing that it yields a product/result.

Ephesians 6:1-3 says, ***"Children, obey your parents in the Lord, for this is right. "Honor your father and mother"—which is the first commandment with a promise— "so that it may go well with you and that you may enjoy long life on the earth."*** As a child, they see that if they obey, it will come with a reward. On the other hand, if they don't obey, the consequence is that they miss out on that reward. As children of God, our obedience to parents shows God we will obey Him. It is unrealistic that we would honor God and we don't see Him, but not the parents we see and have a physical experience with them on a day to day basis. God teaches us how to reverence His authority, by giving us practice with our earthly parents. God doesn't look at it as if we honor Him we will also honor our parents. No, God gave us parents to honor first, which, in turn, honors Him. Why? Because God is not a God of disorder (1 Corinthians 14:33).

Our obedience works its way up, not down the chain of command. This is why God was so serious when He would tell His people to teach His Laws to their children. Why? Because they would be the next generation and what was put in them early would be put into practice/action, later! Deuteronomy 6:6-7 says, ***"These commandments that I give you today are to be on your hearts. Impress them on your children. Talk about them when you sit at home and when you walk along the road, when you lie down and when you get up."*** God knew that the more they talked about the commandments and the more relevant and present the commandments were, that neither them nor their children would forget to obey His Laws. God also knew that if they were in their heart, they would love them enough to be intentional about doing them.

More importantly, it is a Proverbs 22:6 lesson, ***"Train up a child in the way he should go: and when he is old, he will not depart from it."*** If you train for anything, what you do becomes a habit. After training for so long, it becomes them, so they can no longer separate from it. God saw this type of character in Abraham. Genesis 18:19, ***"For I know him, that he will command his children and his household after him, and they shall keep the way of the LORD, to do justice and judgment; that the LORD may bring upon Abraham that which He hath spoken of him."*** Genesis 18:19 means that Abraham was leading the way and being the example of what he commanded to his family. God knew that Abraham wasn't just going to tell his children something he wasn't doing himself, but would lead them by example! Since God could trust Abraham in this way, He was going to keep His Word to him.

Student Teacher:

The person who creates a recipe will demonstrate the best version of it, because they know what led them to the desired outcome. God is the best Demonstrator for us in all aspects, but especially as a Father. That's the way we should be for our children. God's love for us as a Father isn't to just say that He's doing it to make us good parents. However, when you experience that, and become a parent, the intention is that you do what was demonstrated and taught to you. As it relates to us and our children, we cannot guarantee that they will all be parents, but we can guarantee that they have to be human beings coexisting with other human beings.

When we raise them, we are not just preparing them for how they should be as parents, but we are raising them to be spiritually and morally sound individuals. So that when they get older, those things translate into whatever they become, especially as a parent. If we do the opposite of that, we are teaching them to be the opposite of what God has called them to be. Earlier, I referenced Proverbs 22:6, discussing how we should train our children in the way they should go. It also relates to what and how we are training them because the amplified version says, ***"Train up a child in the way he should go [teaching him to seek God's wisdom and will for his abilities and talents], Even when he is old he will not depart from it."*** As parents, we train our children by what they see us do. As children of

God, we should do what we see the Father doing, and as parents, we should repeat what we see the Father doing. Basically, you go from student to student-teacher, where you repeat the steps of the recipe to your children, which were demonstrated to you by the Father.

Even Jesus was a Student-Teacher in that He did what He saw the Father do. John 5:17-21 says, ***"But Jesus answered them, My Father worketh hitherto, and I work. Therefore the Jews sought the more to kill him, because He not only had broken the sabbath, but said also that God was His Father, making Himself equal with God. Then answered Jesus and said unto them, Verily, verily, I say unto you, The Son can do nothing of Himself, but what He seeth the Father do: for what things soever He doeth, these also doeth the Son likewise. For the Father loveth the Son, and sheweth Him all things that Himself doeth: and He will shew Him greater works than these, that ye may marvel. For as the Father raiseth up the dead, and quickeneth them; even so the Son quickeneth whom He will."*** Jesus taught His disciples only what He saw His Father do.

Jesus didn't try to deviate from what He saw His Father doing and add His own spice to it because He knew that if He did it, there would be a consequence. The first reason why there would be consequences if Jesus did His own thing, is because Jesus would've been teaching them to disobey God's authority. The other reason is because if you do the recipe the wrong way, you pass that onto someone else. For parents, if we teach our children the wrong thing, they not only repeat the wrong thing, but they pass that behavior on to their children and those connected to them. That is a very heavy offense with God. Matthew 18:6 says, ***"But whoever causes one of these little ones who believe in Me to sin, it would be better for him to have a great millstone fastened around his neck and to be drowned in the depth of the sea."***

This is a bit extreme for a parent, because I know God gives us grace when we make mistakes, but there are some who are blatantly disregarding the recipe God demonstrated to them as their Father and passing it on to their children! They are knowingly doing the opposite of what was taught to them, doing their own thing, and this behavior is getting passed on from one generation to the next! Any recipes (the Word) God has ever given has never changed and even after all these years, He never modified one Word that He's said. So why teach your children a modified recipe? God specifically commands us in Deuteronomy 4:2, ***"Ye shall not add unto the word which I command you, neither shall ye diminish ought from it, that ye may keep the commandments of the LORD your God which I command you."***

Do you think that you can add or take away something from God's Word (recipe) that would make it better? It's an arrogant thing to think that because Luke 6:40 says, ***"The student is not above the teacher, but everyone who is fully trained will be like their teacher."*** The B part of Luke 6:40 says that, ***"everyone who is fully trained will be like their teacher."*** God is trying to get us to be like Him and we will if we follow His recipe. If this is too deep for you spiritually, just remember to look at it from a natural perspective. We will get into this more later, but we are the cooks who follow the Executive Chef's recipe. We can't get arrogant and think we are these amazing cooks without acknowledging there was an amazing recipe created, that we were taught. We have to stop labeling our children as rebellious or disobedient, if we are being rebellious or disobedient to the recipe (the Word) and they're simply following our lead.

Children can be impressionable, so if they are watching us as parents not uphold the standards that we expect them to uphold, maybe they aren't rebellious/disobedient. Maybe the best way to describe it is that they are misguided by our hypocrisy. I know that's a hard truth, but it was also one I had to come to realize. Matthew 23:1-4 says, ***"Then Jesus said to the crowds and to His disciples: "The teachers of the law and the Pharisees sit in Moses' seat. So you must be careful to do everything they tell you. But do not do what they do, for they do not practice what they preach. They tie up heavy, cumbersome loads and put them on other people's shoulders, but they themselves are not willing to lift a finger to move them."*** Jesus said that the pharisees were requiring people to do things that they wouldn't do themselves.

The pharisees were hypocrites because they expected everyone else to do what they not only didn't do, but couldn't do themselves. If I tell my children that they shouldn't lie to me, they shouldn't hear me on the phone lying to people. As a matter of fact, we shouldn't get our children to lie for us either, and expect them not to realize that they have been trained to do the same to you or others. I'm not trying to blame us parents for everything, because if a parent is having trouble with their child being integrous, it could be something they picked up at school or elsewhere. On the other hand, they could also be mimicking what is being taught to them through their parent's actions. If Jesus said He did only what He saw the Father do, this is not a stretch to think that a child's behavior could come from what they see their parents do.

Going back to Matthew 23:1-3 says, ***"Then Jesus said to the crowds and to His disciples: "The teachers of the law and the Pharisees sit in Moses' seat. So you must be careful to do everything they tell you. But do not do what they do, for they do not practice what they preach."*** Jesus told the crowd and His disciples that they should do what the Pharisees said as it pertained to obeying the Law because the Law was correct. However, Jesus told them they should not follow what the pharisees were doing because they didn't practice what they preach. Jesus told them to obey the Law, but not to follow the rebellion of the Pharisees. We have to understand that sowing seed isn't just financial, but it's also relational. I understand more now how what I sow can show up in my children's behavior later, good or bad. Galatians 6:7 says, ***"Be not deceived; God is not mocked: for whatsoever a man soweth, that shall he also reap."***

I can't expect to reap a harvest of obedience from my children if I am disobedient as a child of God! When I'm ready to call my child's behavior disobedience when I am correcting them, I can almost hear God speaking through me to my child. The only issue is, I hear Him speaking to me, by what I am saying to my children. Luke 6:41-42 says, ***"Why do you look at the speck of sawdust in your brother's eye and pay no attention to the plank in your own eye? How can you say to your brother, 'Brother, let me take the speck out of your eye,' when you yourself fail to see the plank in your own eye? You hypocrite, first take the plank out of your eye, and then you will see clearly to remove the speck from your brother's eye."*** As a child I've heard adults say, *"Do as I say, not as I do."* I don't know if I always thought this as a child, but the older I got, it made no sense to me how adults raised their children.

There is nowhere in scripture that God or Jesus told anyone that they should only do what They said and not as They did. Everything that Jesus did was for an example of how to do something they were going to be asked to do. John 13:14-15 says, ***"If I then, your Lord and Master, have washed your feet; ye also ought to wash one another's feet. For I have given you an example, that ye should do as I have done to you."*** As a parent, we shouldn't set expectations for our children to do anything that we haven't first demonstrated in our actions as to how to do it. You want to know why? Because Jesus didn't do that to us. He demonstrated every single recipe He gave us from the Father, so we don't have an excuse. Imagine Jesus telling His disciples what to do and never demonstrating it to them. It would be difficult to do, I don't care how steadfast you are! If this has been a struggle, the good news is that this is not something that can't be corrected.

Even if we start late in the game, we should let our children see that we believe God's Word so much that we are willing to live by it going forward. Disclaimer: Remember, if you don't get the desired results, you don't blame the recipe, blame the one who didn't execute it correctly. If the parent (teacher) is training the child (student) wrong, the student becomes like their teacher. This is what Jesus was talking about in Matthew 23:15, which says, ***"Woe unto you, scribes and Pharisees, hypocrites! for ye compass sea and land to make one proselyte, and when he is made, ye make him twofold more the child of hell than yourselves."*** If you've truly experienced God as a Father, there are no flaws in His parenting. We shouldn't try to change anything about what Jesus is showing us when we begin raising children, because you contribute to the problem when His recipe teaches us to raise solutions!

Some of us try rushing into becoming parents (teachers) when we haven't been good students ourselves! James 3:1-2 says, ***"Not many of you should become teachers, my fellow believers, because you know that we who teach will be judged more strictly. We all stumble in many ways. Anyone who is never at fault in what they say is perfect, able to keep their whole body in check."*** God gives us so much grace, especially as students because we are still learning. However, when we become parents, we have a greater responsibility, because we are supposed to raise our children in the way they should. Why? Because they are vulnerable and only know what they are taught. We definitely shouldn't rush into teaching (parenting), if we are rebellious or disobedient students. We should spend as much time being the best student we can be. The more we cling to His teachings, the more we will be like our Teacher, which is our Father.

This will in turn prepare us to be the best teachers (parents) ever, because the best teachers demonstrate what they know. I am not saying that we shouldn't have kids until we have this perfect, because God's timing is perfect. What I am saying is we shouldn't be in a rush to mislead someone, especially children, if we aren't going to lead according to the Word of God! If you know better, you're supposed to do better. When I say better, I mean in the sense that if better is what you're supposed to do, you do it! James 4:17, ***"If anyone, then, knows the good they ought to do and doesn't do it, it is sin for them."*** It's a difference between children doing something that's wrong out of ignorance and doing something that they knew they shouldn't have done in the first place.

If they are ignorant of the wrong they've done, maybe they won't get in as much trouble, but it should still be brought to their attention that it's wrong so they don't do it again. However, if they knew what they did and they decided to do it anyway, there is a consequence waiting on them that will hopefully prevent them from doing it again. Luke 12:47 says, ***"That servant who knows his master's will but does not get ready or follow his instructions will be beaten with many blows."*** I am in no way saying to abuse your children, I am saying correct them the way that the bible tells us to correct them, so that they know there is a consequence for knowing that something is wrong and still choosing to do it! 2 Peter 2:21 says, ***"For it had been better for them not to have known the way of righteousness, than, after they have known it, to turn from the holy commandment delivered unto them."***

My oldest was an only child for about two years. As she got older and knew better, I was going to check her about what she knew better than to do. Unfortunately, to her it appeared like she was the only one being corrected and her siblings didn't get disciplined. I had to explain to my oldest once or twice that when she was the age of her younger siblings, she received the same grace, but since she got older and knew better and did the opposite, there would be correction. Matthew 7:24-25 says, ***"Therefore whosoever heareth these sayings of mine, and doeth them, I will liken him unto a wise man, which built his house upon a rock: and the rain descended, and the floods came, and the winds blew, and beat upon that house; and it fell not: for it was founded upon a rock."*** Matthew 7:24-25 says that the wise man is the one who does what Jesus says. This man, although destruction came, he was protected from it because he obeyed Jesus' sayings.

If you aren't wise in doing what you are told to do, what the wise man avoided, you will be exposed to. Matthew 7:26-27 says, ***"And every one that heareth these sayings of mine, and doeth them not, shall be likened unto a foolish man, which built his house upon the sand: And the rain***

descended, and the floods came, and the winds blew, and beat upon that house; and it fell: and great was the fall of it." If we haven't always been those types of teachers (parents) to our kids (students), because we weren't those types of students (children of God) to our Father, don't worry!!! The good news is that it's not too late to become a better student in order to become a better teacher. Even as parents, we are still students. This is the best position as a parent because as you learn better, you should do better so that you can give your children the best recipe for success!

Psalms 127:3 says, ***"Lo, children are an heritage of the LORD: and the fruit of the womb is His reward."***

CHEF VS. COOK Chapter 12.

Kingdom and Kitchen:

This book uses a lot of analogies and one of those things is making a parallel between recipes and God's Word. If you are following a recipe, there must be a place that you learn and use that recipe, which is the kitchen. For this section, we will liken the kitchen to the Kingdom of God, because this is where God has placed His people to implement those recipes. **Disclaimer: I am a visual person and I was given this analogy by the Holy Spirit to hopefully help make sense of our roles between us, God, and His Kingdom. This is simply an analogy and there is nothing exact about it. Just similarities.** Before we get started, I will introduce some titles that I will go into more detail about later. For now, I will only mention them. There will be comparisons between the role of Executive Chef and God, Jesus and the Sous Chef, and us as cooks.

I am not exactly familiar with Gordon Ramsay, but I know there is a show where he shows up in kitchens and invokes change. The purpose of his visit is because the current state of that kitchen was contrary to the original intent of the kitchen. If the kitchen is a disaster, ultimately it affects the restaurant. His job was to get them to a place where the kitchen functions according to its purpose, for the benefit of its consumer. It reminds me of how, in the New Testament, Jesus comes on the scene, talking about the Kingdom of God. He taught His disciples to not have the mindset of the world, but the mindset of those who are a part of the

Kingdom of God. He was teaching them to operate in the Kingdom, according to its original intent. In order for that to happen, they had to have a Kingdom mindset. You would think God in the flesh would have a huge ego, but a Kingdom mindset is one of humility, meekness, and lowliness.

In Matthew 11:29 Jesus says, ***"Take My yoke upon you, and learn from Me, for I am gentle and lowly in heart, and you will find rest for your souls."*** Jesus washed His disciples feet, served God's people, and died for something He didn't do, just to save us. He did all of that to demonstrate how you should serve people, no matter your title or position. On the contrary, in the world, if you are in a high position, it is very easy and sometimes encouraged to have an ego. It does not matter how common or accepted egos with high positions are; in the Kingdom of God, there is no room for them. Matthew 5:5 says, ***"Blessed are the meek: for they shall inherit the earth."*** You would think a ruler of a rich country would beat out all other rulers to inherit the earth, but Jesus said it will be those who are meek.

This does not mean they are not strong, but they are patient, mild-mannered, gentle, and most importantly, their strength is under control. There are times when people will think that their role or position should be elevated. For instance, there were two brothers whose mother thought that her sons deserved to be more than just disciples. She asked for them to be promoted to a greater position of sharing the same role as Jesus (Sous Chef). In Matthew 20:25-27, ***"Jesus***

called them together and said, "You know that the rulers of the Gentiles lord it over them, and their high officials exercise authority over them. Not so with you. Instead, whoever wants to become great among you must be your servant, and whoever wants to be first must be your slave—". It may not make sense to others, but those in "leadership" in the Kingdom of God don't lord their position over people... At least they shouldn't. Instead, they operate as servant-leaders.

Our impact in the Kingdom of God is not in having the highest title, but in how we serve others. Even in Jesus' leadership position, He knew that His role was not to dictate, but to serve. He said Himself in Matthew 20:28, ***"just as the Son of Man did not come to be served, but to serve, and to give his life as a ransom for many."*** When we see this humility in Jesus, it should inspire us to take on the same mindset. In the kitchen, it may seem that the only job of the cook is to prepare meals that feed the consumer. However, that meal is so important because Jesus was serious about feeding the hungry spiritually and physically as well as giving drink to the thirsty spiritually and physically. John 6:35, ***"Jesus said to them, "I am the Bread of life; whoever comes to Me shall not hunger, and whoever believes in Me shall never thirst."***

The reason people are in a restaurant is to be fed and the cooks fulfill that need. Those in leadership in the kitchen are the Executive and the Sous Chef. It is not that the Executive and Sous Chef cannot cook, but it is your gift of cooking that God desires to use in the kitchen to fulfill the needs of the consumer in the restaurant. If I could say it another way, I would say, *"It's not that God or Jesus can't do it themselves, but He desires to use your gift in the Kingdom of God, to fulfill the needs of His people in the world."* People may or may not know this, but they are not just hungry for physical food, but for the Bread of Heaven, which is Jesus. He is the meal that we are offering to them. When Jesus was about to get promoted (ascend back to Heaven) and pass on the leadership role, He had to teach Peter how to lead. He admonished Peter to demonstrate his love for Him, by serving His people.

John 21:15 says, ***"When they had finished breakfast, Jesus said to Simon Peter, "Simon, son of John, do you love Me more than these?" He said to Him, "Yes, Lord; you know that I love you." He said to him, "Feed My lambs."*** You have to love what you do because it requires that you give yourself in service. I will also say that there has to be balance with this. When Jesus needed time to Himself to pray and refresh, He did that. When He saw the woman at the well, he told her to give Him water before He ever offered her the Living Waters. This means that when He felt drained, He did what he needed to do in order to go back and serve. When Jesus had a need (in His flesh) He asked that it be filled before He did anything else. The key to it was balance, so that He wouldn't do anything empty because you can't give what you don't have. This is sometimes our issue.

We lose sight of what's important when we begin to only think about ourselves and what we need. Every cook's thought process must be, *"Prepare what they (consumer) need, and my needs will be taken care of."* Matthew 6:33 says, ***"But seek first the Kingdom of God and His righteousness, and all these things will be added to you."*** We don't have to try to take care of our own needs, because God will do that. We just need to take care of God's people and He will make sure that we lack nothing. Let me help make this make sense. In the natural, if the cook prepares what the consumer needs, their needs are provided for because they will be compensated for their work. In the spiritual, when we take care of the needs of others, we are blessed because of it.

Matthew 25:34-40 says, ***"Then shall the King say unto them on His right hand, Come, ye blessed of My Father, inherit the Kingdom prepared for you from the foundation of the world: For I was an hungred, and ye gave Me meat: I was thirsty, and ye gave Me drink: I was a stranger, and ye took Me in: Naked, and ye clothed Me: I was sick, and ye visited Me: I was in prison, and ye came unto Me. Then shall the righteous answer Him, saying, Lord, when saw we Thee an hungred, and fed Thee? or thirsty, and gave Thee drink? When saw we Thee a stranger, and took Thee in? or naked, and clothed Thee? Or when saw we Thee sick, or in prison, and came unto Thee? And the King shall answer and say unto them, Verily I say unto you, Inasmuch as ye have done it unto one of the least of these My brethren, ye have done it unto Me."*** Every need that we have, being in God's Kingdom, is and has been taken care of. Therefore, we should seek who God wants us to serve in His Kingdom.

This revelation comes with a relationship with Christ. In the case of the kitchen, Jesus is the Sous Chef. Why? Because the Sous Chef tells us what we need to know from the Executive Chef (God). Jesus also teaches us how to communicate with God. Jesus taught us that we communicate with God through prayer, but there was a certain way we needed to talk to Him in order to get what we needed or wanted. In prayer, we aren't asking God for ourselves or for our will to happen. We speak to God, with Whom we have a relationship with (Our Father) and pray on the behalf of not just ourselves but others as well. More importantly, we are asking for His will to be done and not our own. Jesus taught us to ask in Matthew 6:10, ***"Your Kingdom come, Your will be done, on earth as it is in heaven."*** We want what God wants to happen and we want His will to reflect in the earth (restaurant). Why? Because

Psalm 24:1 says, ***"The earth is the LORD's, and the fulness thereof; the world, and they that dwell therein."*** The earth (restaurant) should represent the One that's over it. That's the importance of us asking God to make happen here on earth, what happens in heaven. God is a God of excellence, so whatever He wants to be done, He wants it to be done in a Spirit of excellence. Whatever we prepare for the consumer, it has to represent the Kingdom of God. Consumers (people) have blamed God for the chaos they see in the restaurant (earth), but it's a misrepresentation of Him and His work. The restaurant (earth) has had bad management that didn't represent His Kingdom (Kitchen) and they are purposely trying to make God's restaurant and what He stands for look bad. However, He has trusted us to represent His Kingdom (Kitchen) correctly in the earth (restaurant).

God has also trusted us to bring in more cooks (disciples) and train them to do in His kitchen (Kingdom) what He has taught us to do. Matthew 28:18-20 says, ***"And Jesus came up and spoke to them, saying, "All authority has been given to Me in heaven and on earth. Go therefore and make disciples of all the nations, baptizing them in the name of the Father and the Son and the Holy Spirit, teaching them to observe all that I commanded you; and lo, I am with you always, even to the end of the age."*** We can not allow the enemy to come in and make a mockery of the things of God. It is our job to do His will and make other disciples that come in and do His will as well. We do this by instruction, but also demonstration. All of this belongs to the Lord and the enemy knows that he only has a short time to have what little rule over the world he has.

Revelations 12:12 says, ***"… for the devil is come down unto you, having great wrath, because he knoweth that he hath but a short time."*** Glory to God, there is coming a day where there won't be anyone who can misrepresent His will or desires in the earth (restaurant) or in the world!!! Revelation 11:15 says, ***"Then the seventh angel blew his trumpet, and there were loud voices in heaven, saying, "The kingdom of the world has become the kingdom of our Lord and of His Christ, and He shall reign forever and ever."***

FAST FOOD VS. RESTAURANT:

We all know that if we had a choice to eat fast food or restaurant style food, we would most likely choose fast food because of its convenience, less upfront cost (initially) and less time. Although we know that the restaurant's food will not only taste better but may even be the healthier choice of the two, we still choose convenience. Going back to the fall of man, satan deceiving Eve would be likened to the fast food experience. Eve made a decision based on the convenience of knowing good and evil for herself and not having to trust God. What seemed more convenient turned out to affect her health dramatically. So much so that they began to die from that moment forward. This is how we are most of the time with our choices.

We want what is quick and easy versus what takes time and may be difficult. Cutting corners seems like the most efficient way of doing things, but at what expense? 1 Samuel 15:22-23 says, ***"And Samuel said, Hath the Lord as great delight in burnt offerings and sacrifices, as in obeying the voice of the Lord? Behold, to obey is better than sacrifice, and to hearken than the fat of rams. For rebellion is as the sin of witchcraft, and stubbornness is as iniquity and idolatry. Because thou hast rejected the word of the Lord, He hath also rejected thee from being king."*** The expense for disobedience for king Saul was costly. He thought obeying God a little bit was the same as obeying Him fully. We often see the benefits of fast food at the moment, but rarely will you find someone thinking long term. The same is true with us when we choose to disobey for the potential convenience.

Unfortunately, what we do not see is that obedience is much easier than the consequences of disobedience. The enemy tried tricking Jesus with a fast food experience too, but it didn't appeal to Him the same way God's gourmet meal did. He could see how unhealthy that choice would be in the end and decided He would rather wait for the healthier meal instead because of its lasting benefits. God never presented us with a fast food experience. He prepared our meals for us with a spirit of excellence. The only time you see God instructing His people to eat in a rush or eating while traveling was when they were escaping their enemies from Egypt. Any other time following that, you see Him prepare tables for us. One of the last things Jesus did corporately with His disciples was sit down and break bread with them.

This meal took time to prepare, but the food that He offered them was not only going to satisfy their hunger, but also give them life. Matthew 26:26-28 says, ***"And as they were eating, Jesus took bread, and blessed it, and brake it, and gave it to the disciples, and said, Take, eat; this is My body. And He took the cup, and gave thanks, and gave it to them, saying, Drink ye all of it; For this is My Blood of the new testament, which is shed for many for the remission of sins."*** Jesus was the only One Who could offer them a meal that had perpetual benefits. There is not one food on this earth, natural or preserved, that can last forever or give you eternal life. The reason fast food is not good is that it is prepared quickly and loses nutritional value.

Everything that the enemy has offered is not to your advantage because it is prepared with unhealthy alternatives and additives. Genesis 3:3-5 says, ***"But of the fruit of the tree which is in the midst of the garden, God hath said, Ye shall not eat of it, neither shall ye touch it, lest ye die. And the serpent said unto the woman, Ye shall not surely die: For God doth know that in the day ye eat thereof, then your eyes shall be opened, and ye shall be as gods, knowing good and evil."*** Have you ever seen a product that is advertised as a healthy product, but you read the ingredients and find out that they are worse than sweet treats?! That's exactly how satan got Eve with his false advertisement. He made something look beneficial when it really was detrimental to their health. Aside from the previous reason provided, another reason it's hard to get things that are healthy in a fast food restaurant is because the food is not fresh.

Fast food items contain a lot of artificial ingredients. Most fast food restaurants do not have cooks who are actually cooking your food fresh, so they do not have the advantage of having chefs to direct them. Jesus knew that His disciples didn't need to be left alone the way cooks in fast food restaurants are because they needed guidance. So in John 14:16, Jesus says, ***"And I will ask the Father, and He will give you another Helper, to be with you forever,".*** Cooks, as gifted as they are, are not chefs. Their job is to fulfill the order, but they may or may not understand what is healthy or what isn't. Fast food restaurants can prepare a meal to satisfy your hunger temporarily, but you will eventually have to pay for it (gas, stomachache, weight gain, etc.). This is why we should get our meals from Jesus.

Revelations 19:9 says, ***"Then the angel said to me, "Write this: Blessed are those who are invited to the wedding supper of the Lamb!" And he added, "These are the true words of God."*** The meal Jesus prepared for us is good for us now and later. This is why having a chef in the kitchen to help prepare these meals is beneficial to the consumer. The Sous Chef can help guide the cook to not only make it correctly but also avoid preparing it in an unhealthy way for the consumer. Matthew 16:6 says, ***"Be careful," Jesus said to them. "Be on your guard against the yeast of the Pharisees and Sadducees."*** In Luke 12:1, Jesus called the yeast of the pharisees, hypocrisy. The King James Version of Matthew 16:6 tells us to beware of the leaven of the pharisees. One of the definitions for leaven from Dictionary.com is, *"an element that produces an altering or transforming influence."*

Jesus warned His cooks to beware of the altering and transformative influence of the pharisees. Their recipes for righteousness were very religious and legalistic. It would keep you from doing wrong, but it would also keep you from a relationship with God! Although they gave these recipes, they didn't follow them themselves. The pharisees wanted to make the people do things that they themselves couldn't do, which is why Jesus called the yeast of the pharisees, hypocrisy.

Matthew 23:2-4 says, ***"The teachers of the law and the Pharisees sit in Moses' seat. So you must be careful to do everything they tell you. But do not do what they do, for they do not practice what they preach. They tie up heavy, cumbersome loads and put them on other people's shoulders, but they themselves are not willing to lift a finger to move them."*** These were bad chefs because they were leading the cooks in the wrong direction. A really good sous' chef knows what is healthy for the people.

Jesus was the best Sous Chef in that He made sure we had the Holy Spirit. There were health benefits living by the Spirit versus living by the flesh. Yeast of the pharisees (hypocrisy) and yeast from bread are both not healthy for us. Paul told us of the health benefits of having more fruit, that is, the fruit of the Spirit, are. Galatians 5:22-24 says, ***"But the fruit of the Spirit is love, joy, peace, forbearance, kindness, goodness, faithfulness, gentleness and self-control. Against such things there is no law. Those who belong to Christ Jesus have crucified the flesh with its passions and desires."*** I love that Paul was specific about which fruit, because although they were warned, the fruit that Adam and Eve ate wasn't specifically identified. So, if God didn't say don't eat of it, they couldn't have known if it was or wasn't healthy for them. They just had to trust Him.

Unfortunately, what they ate would take us years to be delivered from. The fruit they ate had side effects that people would have if they had a certain medication. It wasn't until Jesus came that we were delivered from that side effect. The enemy's scheme with fast food is trying to get you to prepare something ignorantly, in a short amount of time that appears to be healthy, but in the end will be detrimental. I heard Jonathan Evans' wife say something like, *"Eating healthy may cost more money, but either you pay for it now or you will pay for it later."* In all honesty, we can have whatever we want, but that doesn't mean that everything will be beneficial to you. Paul says in 1 Corinthians 10:23 says, ***"I have the right to do anything," you say—but not everything is beneficial. "I have the right to do anything"—but not everything is constructive.*** He says something similar in 1 Corinthians 6:12, ***"Everything is permissible for me," but not everything is beneficial. "Everything is permissible for me," but I will not be mastered by anything."***

This is why having guidance is so important to our spiritual and physical health! If we are taught that everything that is prepared or promised to happen quickly is not always God's plan/best for us we would be able to beat the enemy at his game. Sometimes, things that are prepared slowly and with attention to detail (following the recipe) are the healthiest and best experiences for us. Every good experience produces a good review (testimony). Revelations 12:11 says, ***"And they overcame him by the blood of the Lamb, and by the word of their testimony;...".*** The benefits of testimony (reviews) is that others will begin to tell people of their experience with God and what He has done for them. The better the reputation of the Kitchen (Kingdom) in that restaurant (earth), the more people will go out into the world and advertise its goodness!!! Matthew

24:14 says, ***"And this Gospel of the Kingdom will be proclaimed throughout the whole world as a testimony to all nations, and then the end will come."***

We can't be content with those closest to us knowing God is good. We must also be concerned about the world. We have to make sure that before it's all over, everyone has had a Psalms 34:8 opportunity to ***"Taste and see that the LORD is good; blessed is the one who takes refuge in Him."*** People can see that this recipe (the Word) is not like anything else and it makes their palette change from desiring what is bad to what is right for them. 1 Peter 2:1-3 says, ***"Therefore, rid yourselves of all malice and all deceit, hypocrisy, envy, and slander of every kind. Like newborn babies, crave pure spiritual milk, so that by it you may grow up in your salvation, now that you have tasted that the Lord is good."*** Everything that they ate before was unhealthy and wasn't good for consumption.

However, God's recipes are not only good to taste, but it is better/healthier for us. The better/healthier you eat, the more you begin to crave the right things.

Chain of Command:

Since we are discussing recipes, let's look at the chain of command in the kitchen. If you go to a restaurant, depending on the type, you will have an executive chef running the kitchen. Zip Recruiter says, *"Executive chefs are the highest level of management in the kitchen..."* Therefore, in our Kitchen (Kingdom) the Executive Chef would represent God, because He is the highest in command. Psalms 97:9 says, ***"For You are the Lord Most High over all the earth; You are exalted far above all gods."*** There is no one above the executive chef, just like there is no one above God, because He is the Most High God. His skills as the highest in command consist of His ability to, *"... create recipes and execute them consistently and quickly ..."* (Zip Recruiter). Genesis 1:1 says, ***"In the beginning God created the heaven and the earth."***

God created the earth (restaurant), but that's not all He created. 2 Timothy 3:16-17 says, ***"All scripture is given by inspiration of God, and is profitable for doctrine, for reproof, for correction, for instruction in righteousness: That the man of God may be perfect, thoroughly furnished unto all good works."*** So we have the Executive Chef (God), who has created the recipes (the Word) for the menu that we will use. Although the executive chef is the highest level of management in the kitchen, they are not the one who carry out the menu. We will discuss later who is responsible for carrying out the menu, but before we discuss them, there is Someone who works between the executive chef and the one who carries out the menu. This person is called the sous chef. The sous chef is responsible for making sure that the recipes on the menu are fulfilled to the executive chef's desire.

According to Escoffier School of Culinary Arts, the sous chefs *"... are called upon to support executive chefs and represent them in their absence."* It says that the sous chef represents the executive chef's absence. The parallel is that Jesus was sent to represent God, not in His absence, because He is everywhere at the same time (omnipresent), but in His invisibility. Colossians 1:15 says, ***"The Son is the image of the invisible God, the Firstborn over all creation."*** In the absence of the executive chef, the sous chef assumes all authority and responsibility. When Jesus came to earth, He assumed the same responsibility in making sure that everything that God (Executive Chef) desired in His Kitchen (Kingdom), came to pass. The sous chef's job is not to make his own vision come to life, but the vision of the executive chef.

John 6:38 says, ***"For I have come down from heaven, not to do My own will, but to do the will of Him Who sent Me."*** That means Jesus' (the Sous Chef) job is to make sure that God (Executive Chef) has the desired atmosphere in His restaurant (earth) and those in the Kitchen (Kingdom) understand how to carry out His menu. Escoffier School of Culinary Arts also said, *"The sous chef often is the one responsible for training new staff members and managing the team."* I will quote 2 Timothy 3:16-17, but from the English Standard Version, which says, ***"All Scripture is breathed out by God and profitable for teaching, for reproof, for correction, and for training in righteousness, that the man of God may be competent, equipped for every good work."*** Scripture is God's Word and the analogy is that the Word is the recipe.

The Sous Chef (Jesus) trains those under Him to know and understand the recipes (the Word) the Executive Chef (God) has created. You find many times in scripture where it says Jesus was teaching His disciples the will of God, training/preparing them for their assignment. Jesus had to teach His disciples the will of the Father (Executive Chef), so that they would know how to correctly fulfill their assignment in the earth (restaurant). There will be times where the sous chef's authority might be in question so it's important that they not only understand their authority, but that they also understand who they are to the executive chef. Mark 11:23 says, ***"By what authority are you doing these things?" they asked. "And who gave you authority to do this?"***

As I stated before, there will be those people questioning the sous chefs because they want to know how much authority they have. The pharisees were the authority, so for Jesus to say He had authority, even over them, was probably a threat to their authority. Jesus answered those questions explaining His authority many times like in John 5:22-23, which says, ***"Moreover, the Father judges no one, but has entrusted all judgment to the Son, that all may honor the Son just as they honor the Father. Whoever does not honor the Son does not honor the Father, Who sent Him."*** It was important for the disciples to understand that Jesus' authority came from God so any resistance to the Sous Chef (Jesus) is resistance to the Executive Chef's (God) orders. Why? Because the Executive Chef (God) gave Jesus that authority to bring to life His vision.

Everything the executive chef demonstrated to the sous chef, is what he in turn demonstrates to the cooks. John 5:19 says, ***"So Jesus replied, "Truly, truly, I tell you, the***

Son can do nothing by Himself, unless He sees the Father doing it. For whatever the Father does, the Son also does." A good sous chef will make sure that what the executive chef wants to happen, happens. Also, a good sous chef makes sure that everything he does is exactly what the executive chef would do if he were actually there. He is not trying to take credit for what is happening because everything he does is identical to what the executive chef does. Everything the disciples were learning from Jesus, was what God showed Jesus.

Jesus wasn't teaching the disciples anything He did Himself. He only taught what He saw God doing. This is why God was so pleased with Jesus as His Son (Sous Chef) because He wasn't trying to do His own thing. He only came to do God's will! John 4:34 says, ***"Jesus saith unto them, My meat is to do the will of Him that sent Me, and to finish His work."*** Jesus led by example because we are also supposed to be here doing the Father's (Executive Chef) will. It was also important for Jesus to make sure that God's work was finished. This is what makes a good sous chef too! He can make sure that whatever the executive chef wants done, it gets completed. The sous chef also knows how to train those under him to make their work mirror that of the executive chef's work, because the sous chef's work mirrors the executive chef's work.

John 10:30 says, ***"I and My Father are One."*** Jesus (Sous Chef) knows the will of the Executive Chef (God) so well, they have become One. John 17:20-23 says, ***"I do not pray for these alone, but also for those who will believe in Me***

through their word; that they all may be one, as You, Father, are in Me, and I in You; that they also may be one in Us, that the world may believe that You sent Me. And the glory which You gave Me I have given them, that they may be one just as We are One: I in them, and You in Me; that they may be made perfect in one, and that the world may know that You have sent Me, and have loved them as You have loved Me." Jesus desired for His disciples to become one with the Father just as He had. Therefore, the sous chef trains those under him so well that they, like him, will become one with executive chef in mind and performance.

Those under the sous chef reflect what the sous chef reflected, which was the executive chef. The point of Jesus' teachings was to bring the disciples into this unique relationship with the Father so that if other people saw Christ in the disciples, they should have also seen God, because that's Who Christ reflected. As we discussed before, the executive chef creates the recipes and menu and passes on the responsibility to the sous chef. The sous chef manages those who will carry out the recipe, which are the cooks. According to Indeed's job description, the cooks, *"... typically follow someone else's recipes or meal plans."* In this analogy, we are the cooks who will carry out the recipes (the Word) on the menu. Being a cook in the natural may seem like a low level position, but it is not a low level position in the natural nor in the spiritual.

You are being trusted with the task of bringing a vision to life and that's a privilege! However, if a person doesn't see their role as significant, they may begin to think of ways to increase their stock in the company. A lot of people will see this as ego, but insecurity is the driving force of self exaltation. Sometimes you can allow those insecurities to make you believe that your role is insignificant when it isn't. Eventually, those insecure thoughts can develop one or two ways: you can fall back and try to play your role, or you can think that you should try to show people who you are. Depending on the intent, both of these are the wrong attitudes to have because the former can make you apathetic and the latter will make you try to alter the recipe just to try to prove that you're more important than the role given.

What if Jesus had that mentality? From the time He was of age, He was a Carpenter for years before He performed His first miracle. No one can tell me the reason He operated in such humility was because He didn't harness that ability before that time. You see in John 2:4 it says, ***"Woman, why do you involve Me?" Jesus replied. "My hour has not yet come."*** Although Jesus said His hour had not come, He still performed His first miracle before it was time. So, since we know that He possessed the ability before it was time, we know that Jesus had to have had a meek and humble mindset while being in the position of a carpenter. So, if our role as a cook seems insignificant in our eyes, we don't understand the process of ascension. Paul warns us in Romans 12:3, which says, ***"For by the grace given me I say to every one of you: Do not think of yourself more highly than you ought, but rather think of yourself with***

sober judgment, in accordance with the faith God has distributed to each of you."
Everything we've been given is from God. Even our faith is given to us! Since the cooks don't create the recipe, it is audacious for them to think or actually change the recipe as they cook. The same with us, we shouldn't get arrogant to think that we are too creative to just stick to God's recipe because the creativity we have comes from the One Who created it. Unfortunately, due to the misconception of the position of the cook, most begin to think that they have to demonstrate their creativity, ability, or knowledge, which causes them to alter the recipe. We don't realize that we are more blessed in our obedience to carry out the menu as stated rather than to prove that we are better than our entrusted assignment. Whatever we do, no matter how good it is, God still makes it better! However, you don't have to change anything about God's Word (the recipe) because it's perfect!

It's perfect because every time it's going to do what God created it to do!!! Isaiah 55:11 says, ***"So shall My word be that goes out from My mouth; it shall not return to Me empty, but it shall accomplish that which I purpose, and shall succeed in the thing for which I sent it."*** All we have to do is follow the recipe (the Word) as given and it will succeed! We shouldn't feel so egotistical to try to jazz up the recipe (the Word), but we should take great honor in that our gifts were chosen to bring the vision to pass. So whatever your assignment is, it should glorify God. The same way the cook's work glorifies the executive chef. Colossians 3:16-17 says, ***"Let the word of Christ dwell in***

you richly, teaching and admonishing one another in all wisdom, singing psalms and hymns and spiritual songs, with thankfulness in your hearts to God. And whatsoever ye do in word or deed, do all in the name of the Lord Jesus, giving thanks to God and the Father by Him."

Everything we do was designed to glorify God. Work, extracurricular activities, parenting, marriage, etc. were all created for the glory of God. So when we do these things, we can do them because we're aware that it's a gift to us and we're just presenting it back to God in gratitude! We don't have to exalt ourselves because our humility in obeying the Father will give us the promotion we really desire!!!

<u>Don't Change the Recipe! It Could Cost You Your Position!</u>

The sous chef never has to exalt himself if he is taking care of his assignment well. Wikipedia says, *"the second in command in a kitchen; the person ranking next after the head chef." Consequently, the sous-chef holds much responsibility in the kitchen, which can eventually lead to promotion to becoming the head chef."* The sous chef's promotion didn't come because he exalted himself, but because he remained humble and obedient to His assignment. Look at what Philippians 2:5-11 says about Jesus, ***"Let this mind be in you, which was also in Christ Jesus: Who, being in the form of God, thought it not robbery to be equal with God: But made Himself of no reputation, and took upon Him the form of a servant, and was made in the likeness of men: And being found in***

fashion as a man, He humbled Himself, and became obedient unto death, even the death of the cross. Wherefore God also hath highly exalted Him, and given Him a name which is above every name: That at the name of Jesus every knee should bow, of things in heaven, and things in earth, and things under the earth; And that every tongue should confess that Jesus Christ is Lord, to the glory of God the Father."

Jesus not only was obedient, but He was humble. His humility and obedience is what gave Him the promotion He received! Jesus didn't allow Himself to feel the need to promote Himself just because He is ⅓ of the Godhead. If Jesus didn't exalt Himself, we shouldn't feel the need to either. Psalms 75:5-7 says, ***"Do not lift your horns against heaven; do not speak so defiantly.'" No one from the east or the west or from the desert can exalt themselves. It is God who judges: He brings one down, he exalts another."*** We don't have to try to exalt ourselves, especially above the sous chef, because if the sous chef moves up, guess what? There is room for the cook who has taken care of his assignment well to move up to. John 14:12-14 says, ***"Truly, truly, I say to you, whoever believes in Me will also do the works that I do; and greater works than these will he do, because I am going to the Father. Whatever you ask in My name, this I will do, that the Father may be glorified in the Son. If you ask Me anything in My name, I will do it."***

The fact that we are "cooks" is a promotion in and of itself because we were slaves to sin and separated from God. We weren't even worthy to come to Him in prayer without the high priest offering a sacrifice on our behalf. Now we are co-heirs with Christ and able to receive the same inheritance as He does. The enemy would love to make us think more highly of ourselves and to try to get us to manipulate the recipe. This reminds me of what happened to Eve. God gave us plenty of options to choose from to eat. Yet, the serpent came in and tried to persuade Eve to question God (Executive Chef) and His infinite wisdom. If he got her to question what God said, he could also get her to alter the "recipe" by adding the fruit from the forbidden tree in the mix. Once the man and woman ate the forbidden fruit, they forfeited their position from "cook" to being kicked out of the garden completely! Humans can be an arrogant bunch.

Rarely do we see how much of a privilege it is to be in communion with the Father. We get so high off of our gifts and talents that we completely forget the fact that God gave them to us. If we were cooks in a kitchen, some of us would find a reason why we should be the one in charge, rather than be grateful that we have an assignment in God's Kitchen (Kingdom) to begin with! It amazes me that the sous chef could be as close to the executive chef and have more humility than the cook, whose only access to the executive chef is through the sous chef. John 14:6-7 says, ***"Jesus answered, "I am the Way and the Truth and the Life. No one comes to the Father except through Me. If you really know Me, you will know My Father as well. From now on, you do know Him and have seen Him."*** Jesus (Sous Chef) is the only Way to the Father, the same way the sous chef is the next step in the chain of command to the executive chef.

The sous chef's directives to the cooks are as good as the executive chef speaking himself. So whatever the sous chef says needs to happen, are not his own, but those of the executive chef's. The sous chef knows this because he is the mediator between the executive chef and the cook. 1 Timothy 2:5 says, ***"For there is One God, and One Mediator between God and men, the Man Christ Jesus;".*** Jesus (Sous Chef) helps us to know the mind of God (Executive Chef) and His desires and how He wants His Kitchen (Kingdom) to run. He also speaks to God on our behalf, communicating our heart and what we need to help us to fulfill His desires in the Kitchen (Kingdom). Order is very important in the kitchen because it determines what gets communicated and what doesn't. There are many people who have this theory that there is more than one way to God and whether they realize it or not, it is the reason for so many prayer requests (orders) being miscommunicated or going unanswered.

Unfortunately some of us try to take all of these different ways we've made up to get to God. When we do this, we are unconsciously saying doing things Christ way isn't the best way. This is where we try to freestyle the recipe because for some strange reason we think we know more than the sous chef and executive chef. Let me ask it like this, why do we think we know more than the Creator and we are His creation? Jesus isn't Lording His authority over us, He's trying to get us promoted. Jesus knew that His promotion meant our promotion and that in the earth we would do greater things than what He did in the earth (restaurant). Jesus has called us to greater and He has also been interceding for us so that God will do what we are asking Him to do. However, we must obey Him to become and get to greater! Deuteronomy 5:33 says, ***"Walk in obedience to all that the Lord your God has commanded you, so that you may live and prosper and prolong your days in the land that you will possess."*** If we want to prosper and have longevity, doing things our way isn't going to work.

We must mature to a place where what we want to do doesn't override what we should do. It's in our maturity that we are able to be obedient and do what is asked of us. If we don't know or understand this, we put ourselves in a position to lose our position. Let's look at two examples that show the humility and obedience of Jesus that got Him His promotion and the arrogance of the prodigal son that made him temporarily lose his spot. Philippians 2:8-11 says, ***"And being found in fashion as a man, He humbled Himself, and became obedient unto death, even the death of the cross. Wherefore God also hath highly exalted Him, and given Him a name which is above every name: That at the Name of Jesus every knee should bow, of things in heaven, and things in earth, and things under the earth; And that every tongue should confess that Jesus Christ is Lord, to the glory of God the Father."***

From the beginning the devil tried to tempt Jesus not to go through the process that would cause Him to be exalted. The devil tried offering Jesus His exaltation sooner, but

Jesus knew that it already belonged to Him, but He would have to be patient to go through the process to get it.That's our biggest problem, impatience! We want what God promised to us, but we don't want to wait on it. Not having to wait seems like an awesome idea, but if we get it before time, there is no longevity or blessing to getting things prematurely. Proverbs 20:21, ***"An inheritance claimed too soon will not be blessed at the end."*** Jesus knew that gaining the world in that moment was getting it illegally and it wasn't going to last in the end. Jesus knew all of this because He had an intimate relationship with God. He knew Psalm 37:9 says, ***"For evildoers shall be cut off: But those that wait upon the LORD, they shall inherit the earth."***

This was an advantage because no matter how good it sounded, Jesus knew that He had an inheritance. He also knew what belonged to Him and Who (God) possessed it to give it to Him. Revelations 11:5 says, ***"And the seventh angel sounded; and there were great voices in heaven, saying, The kingdoms of this world are become the kingdoms of our Lord, and of His Christ; and He shall reign for ever and ever."*** On the other hand, the prodigal son didn't have that relationship to know the outcome. Luke 15:12-14 says, ***"And the younger of them said to his father, Father, give me the portion of goods that falleth to me. And he divided unto them his living. And not many days after the younger son gathered all together, and took his journey into a far country, and there wasted his substance with riotous living. And when he had spent all,***

there arose a mighty famine in that land; and he began to be in want."

The prodigal son was also aware that he had an inheritance. The only issue was waiting on the time he was supposed to receive it. When he received his inheritance sooner, the same principle applied on how long it would last. The prodigal son's inheritance was short lived and he lived an unnecessarily difficult life because of it. We put ourselves through unnecessary hardship simply because we don't want to wait. Fortunately, the prodigal son realized that he didn't have to live that way and went back to his father. When we finally come to ourselves and repent, our merciful God welcomes us back. Although the prodigal son returned home, it doesn't tell us in scripture if he received another inheritance when it was finally time to receive it. Either way, I am sure he was grateful that he was no longer in the place he was in prior to returning home.

There will always be benefits to waiting on God. Psalm 37:34 says, ***"Wait on the LORD, and keep His way, and He shall exalt thee to inherit the land: When the wicked are cut off, thou shalt see it."*** I spoke about the temporary gain of getting what God promised before time, but there is also demotion. Isaiah 14:14-15 says, ***"You said in your heart, "I will ascend to the heavens; I will raise my throne above the stars of God; I will sit enthroned on the mount of assembly, on the utmost heights of Mount Zaphon. I will ascend above the tops of the clouds; I will make myself like the Most High." But you are brought down to the realm of the dead, to the depths of the pit."*** We see that lucifer spent more time thinking about how good he could do God's job, rather than his own. Rather than taking care of the assignment he was given, he chose to focus on the position he wanted. Therefore, he lost the position completely and was demoted to the lowest position possible. He can't even get his position back!

The devil has been jealous of our position ever since and has tried to get us to make the same decision he made. However, we can't allow the enemy to talk us into trying to promote ourselves and trick us right out of our position again! If his advice works so well, why didn't it work for him? Fortunately, God sent His Son (Sous Chef), the last Adam to come and put the restaurant (earth) back in order! When Eve was tempted by the serpent, she and Adam fell because of their decision. So in order for us to not be beguiled and lose our position again, we must spend time with God. The more time you spend with God, the more you get to know Him. John 17:3 says, ***"And this is eternal life, that they know You the only true God, and Jesus Christ whom You have sent."***

Jesus's knowledge of the Father helped Him not only maintain His position, but to also be promoted. He knew what the Father was going to give Him, so He knew everything satan offered wasn't legit. Our greatest defense against the devil is knowing what God said. The Sous Chef is there to help you fulfill the desires of the Executive Chef. He doesn't get anything out of your failure, so He is making sure that He leads you according to Psalms 23:3, ***"in the paths of righteousness for his name's sake."*** Why? Because His Name is on it! We are in one of the most prestigious positions being co-heirs with Christ because we share the inheritance with Him. Ephesians 2:4-6 says, ***"But God, who is rich in mercy, for his great love wherewith he loved us, Even when we were dead in sins, hath quickened us together with Christ, (by grace ye are saved;) And hath raised us up together, and made us sit together in heavenly places in Christ Jesus:"***.

The same with the cooks. They are just as much like the sous chef because they do what the sous chef can do, which is do what the executive chef desires. That means that the sous chef is like the executive chef as well! Unfortunately, Eve allowed someone who wasn't the "Executive Chef" to make her believe she could gain something she already had, by doing something God forbade her to do. This one decision didn't get her the promotion she wanted. Instead, it cost her and Adam their position. They lost the opportunity to walk and talk with God, their place in the Garden, and went from eternal life, to slowly dying. Talk about a demotion! We may not always get it right and God knows that, but I love that God is gracious enough that even if we got something out of His timing, He gives us another opportunity to have it when we are ready for it.

During that time, He allows us to grow in patience, humility, and obedience, in order to prepare us for what He has promised to us. Paul explained this in Philemon 1:15, which says, ***"Perhaps the reason he was separated from you for a little while was that you might have him back forever".*** We were separated from God for a season, but Jesus not only brought us back to God, but through His act of obedience, He bought back a freedom we forfeited years ago. We now have access to the Father and the hope of everlasting life with God like we did before. If we are patient enough, God will not only give us what He promised us, but the longevity to go with it! That longevity is called eternal life! All we have to do is follow Jesus' lead. He didn't try to think more highly of Himself, even though He had a reason to. Jesus' humility to obey and serve God got Him elevated. We should give God glory because Christ obedience exalted Him to a position that we are able to be promoted to with Him.

I want to reiterate Ephesians 2 again, this time verses 4-9, which says, ***"But God, Who is rich in mercy, for His great love wherewith He loved us, Even when we were dead in sins, hath quickened us together with Christ, (by grace ye are saved;) And hath raised us up together, and made us sit together in heavenly places in Christ Jesus: That in the ages to come He might shew the exceeding riches of His grace in His kindness toward us through Christ Jesus. For by grace are ye saved through faith; and that not of yourselves: it is the gift of God: Not of works, lest any man should boast."*** We can't think highly of ourselves because that position was totally by grace and not because of anything we did! This promotion is available, but we have to have the same mindset as Christ does. The motivation is that if we don't obey and serve God with the same mindset as Christ, we will find ourselves in the same position as lucifer trying to exalt ourselves and losing our position.

One of the reasons lucifer lost his position was not just self exaltation, but because he obviously couldn't handle authority. For any cook, if the sous chef is giving you directives, it's not coming from him, it's coming from the executive chef. The same is true with us. If Christ is our Guide, we must not rebel against Him because we would be rebelling against God. Romans 13:1-2 says, ***"Let everyone be subject to the governing authorities, for there is no authority except that which God has established. The authorities that exist have been established by God. Consequently, whoever rebels against the authority is rebelling against what God has instituted, and those who do so will bring judgment on themselves."*** This is what happened when people began to rebel against Moses, not realizing their rebellion wasn't against what Moses said, but against what God said.

For cooks, their rebellion could cause them to lose their job. For those in the wilderness with Moses, their punishment was more severe. Some died when the earth swallowed them up, others died by plague and their disobedience cost them being able to enter into the Promised Land! I am grateful to God that He gives us His grace that death is not the penalty, but it is still important that we get away from the rebellious mindset that in order for us to be great, we must only rule and never submit or obey. If this has been your problem, don't worry, the Word (recipe) teaches us what to do to correct it. Let's allow ourselves to take on a new mindset that obedience and humility is the key to our exaltation and success in the Kitchen (Kingdom).

Luke 6:40 says, ***"The disciple is not above his master: but every one that is perfect shall be as his master."***

CHANGE AGENT Chapter 13.

Now that we've identified the problem, it's imperative that we identify the solution. The Decision Lab says, *"A change agent is a group or individual who is able to tackle an organization's problem from a behavioral perspective and understand the nuances of how to mobilize change."* I absolutely LOVE this definition for where we are going because it links the problem with the source of the problem, which is behavior. The reason I titled the book *"You're the Problem, not the Recipe"*, is because of the behavior, not necessarily the person. When we have displayed behaviors long enough, we begin to identify with them and say things like, *"This is who I am."* However, that is not true. Every "problem" that is discussed in each chapter is based on the behavior that you are displaying towards that particular thing.

The New International Version of Romans 7:15-20 says, ***"I do not understand what I do. For what I want to do I do not do, but what I hate I do. And if I do what I do not want to do, I agree that the law is good. As it is, it is no longer I myself who do it, but it is sin living in me. For I know that good itself does not dwell in me, that is, in my sinful nature. For I have the desire to do what is good, but I cannot carry it out. For I do not do the good I want to do, but the evil I do not want to do—this I keep on doing. Now if I do what I do not want to do, it is no longer I who do it, but it is sin living in me that does it."*** I'm sure you're probably still asking, *"Well why would you name your book* *that?"* Well, it's because we confuse our behavior with who we are, or better yet, we confuse our behavior with who God said we are. How you act is not who you are, but it is who everyone gets to meet. So if the you we are presented with is contrary to the Word of God (recipe), you are the problem and not the recipe. Think about it, marriage, ministry, parenting, etc. were created by a perfect God, with Jesus as the perfect Example, with flawed individuals operating in each one.

So, how can His perfection be the problem? We can make the excuse all day long that we aren't perfect, but we will never have the excuse that we don't have a blueprint to know how to effectively do it! We will always be the problem if we always have the same mindset. It's not until we change our mindset that we will change our behavior. Romans 12:2 says, ***"And be not conformed to this world: but be ye transformed by the renewing of your mind, that ye may prove what is that good, and acceptable, and perfect, will of God."***

The New Living Translation says, ***"Don't copy the behavior and customs of this world, but let God transform you into a new person by changing the way you think. Then you will learn to know God's will for you, which is good and pleasing and perfect."*** Remember, a perfect God, gave us a perfect Savior, Who is the perfect Example of how to respond in every area of life. So the reason you have a problem in any of these areas is that you've taken on the mindset of the world. You've adopted the world's customs and ways of thinking, while believing God for each one of those areas to get better. Basically, you want the world's recipe, with God's results, and you have the audacity to be upset with God when it does not work. As long as you think like the world, that will be the way you respond. The change has to come in the area that you are getting your information from, the mind. God's Word tells us to be transformed by the renewing of our mind. Therefore, in order to get better results, we must start in the mind.

Change Your Mind, Change You:

When we don't get God's results, we immediately cast blame on Him as if He hasn't come through on His promises. The truth of the matter is, we've adopted behaviors and ways of thinking that keep us from seeing His promises (desired results). Paul says this in Ephesians 4:22-24, ***"You were taught, with regard to your former way of life, to put off your old self, which is being corrupted by its deceitful desires; to be made new in the attitude of your minds; and to put on the new self, created to be like God in true righteousness and holiness."*** Putting off the old self isn't changing your clothes or hairstyle, but your old way of thinking. The bonus is that when your mindset changes, everything begins to mirror that, from your behavior to your appearance. When we put off the old to put on the new self, that is the self that is created to be like God. So what does it actually mean to change our minds?

Acts 3:19 says, ***"Repent ye therefore, and be converted, that your sins may be blotted out, when the times of***

refreshing shall come from the presence of the Lord;". What does repent mean? Bible Study Tools defines the word repent as, *"To change one's mind & purpose; regret."* If we are going to be change agents, we can't have the same mindset we had before. We have to have a changed mind, if the mind we had before was producing undesired outcomes. Our behavior stems from the way we think. If how we thought before was carnal, then we will live a life that reflects those thoughts. However, when we repent, we change our minds, which should reflect behavior like the One we were created to have.

Changed Mind, Reveals His Will:

The other important thing about changing our mind is we know what His will is for our life. Remember, Romans 12:2 says, ***"And be not conformed to this world: but be ye transformed by the renewing of your mind, that ye may prove what is that good, and acceptable, and perfect, will of God."*** A lot of times I question what God's will is, but I've heard Dr. Myles Munroe say that, *"God's will is His Word and His Word is His will."* Which made me just think of Isaiah 55:10-11, which says, ***"For as the rain cometh down, and the snow from heaven, and returneth not thither, but watereth the earth, and maketh it bring forth and bud, that it may give seed to the sower, and bread to the eater: So shall My Word be that goeth forth out of My mouth: it shall not return unto Me void, but it shall accomplish that which I please, and it shall prosper in the thing whereto I sent it."*** This means that whatever God has said in His Word, it's not what He hopes to come to pass, but what WILL come to pass. Why? Because His Word is His will, and might I add, His will is perfect!

So how do we know His will outside of us understanding His Word? Renewing our mind helps us to know what is that good, acceptable, and perfect will of God is. 1 Corinthians 2:16 says, ***"For who hath known the mind of the Lord, that he may instruct Him? but we have the mind of Christ."*** Let's make sure we understand what the word renewed means. It means, *"having been resumed, re-established, or revived."* This means there was a mindset that we had before, but something changed it, and now, we need to re-establish that mindset. That mind is the mind of Christ which helps direct us in our lives because we know His thoughts and purpose for us. As it pertains to His recipe (the Word), God's will are the desired results/outcome of every recipe He's given. So when we follow His recipe (the Word), we see His will (the desired results) for our lives manifest.

Oxford defines a will as, *"a legal declaration of a person's wishes regarding the disposal of his or her property or estate after death"*. God had a will prepared well before the death of Jesus and He came to fulfill the articles in that will. John 6:38-40 says, ***"For I came down from heaven, not to do Mine own will, but the will of Him that sent Me. And this is the Father's will which hath sent Me, that of all which He hath given Me I should lose nothing, but should raise it up again at the last day. And this is the will of Him that sent Me, that every one which seeth the Son, and believeth on Him, may have everlasting life: and I***

will raise him up at the last day. Outside of the land and property that belonged to the LORD (Psalms 24:1), His investments were one of His main concerns. That investment was our life and Jesus came to do the Father's will, which was saving us in this life so that we would live life eternally with Him. God not only sent Jesus to die for us so that we will have eternal life, but while we were here living, we would live it more abundantly.

John 10:10 tells us, ***"The thief cometh not, but for to steal, and to kill, and to destroy: I am come that they might have life, and that they might have it more abundantly."*** The way Jesus made sure that we would have life more abundantly was that it wouldn't be spent lacking because of the debts we accumulated. Wills are designed to leave something behind to help make a loved one's life better or easier so that they do not have the burden of debt. So anyone who leaves behind a will wants to make sure that when they receive their inheritance, all debts are canceled. Colossians 2:13-15 says, ***"And you, being dead in your sins and the uncircumcision of your flesh, hath He quickened together with Him, having forgiven you all trespasses; Blotting out the handwriting of ordinances that was against us, which was contrary to us, and took it out of the way, nailing it to His cross; And having spoiled principalities and powers, He made a shew of them openly, triumphing over them in it."***

Verse 14 in the New International Version says, ***"having canceled the charge of our legal indebtedness, which stood against us and condemned us; He has taken it away,***

nailing it to the cross." You have to understand that what you inherit from Jesus' will is not going to be based on anything we did or would do, but solely on what He did. 1 Peter 2:24 says, ***"He Himself bore our sins in His body on the tree, so that we might die to sin and live to righteousness. "By His stripes you are healed."*** God's will was that Jesus would die so that we might live and live a life in full, not in debt. From living a life to the glory of God on this side of heaven, we get to the next benefit of God's will, which is eternal life when we transition! Romans 6:23 says, ***"For the wages of sin is death, but the free gift of God is eternal life in Christ Jesus our Lord."***

It's important that we know the ultimate will and gift of God is eternal life with the Triune God (God the Father, God the Son, and God the Holy Spirit). Jesus didn't want us to just have life, or just have a full debt free life, but He also wanted us to have life beyond this life and have it forever! John 10:28-30 says, ***"I give them eternal life, and they shall never perish; no one will snatch them out of My hand. My Father, Who has given them to Me, is greater than all; no one can snatch them out of My Father's hand. I and the Father are One."*** Since the Father and the Son are One, Their will for our life is the same. That will is that we inherit something no one could take away from us, that would give us a better life and future.

Be Transformed By A Renewed Mind:

We discussed the benefits of having a renewed mind of Christ. On the contrary, when we have the mindset of the world, we begin to deviate from the recipe. Therefore, we never see God's will for our life. We simply see a failed version of what He desired for us. There is a song that says, *"The world is ever changing",* and since that is true, we have to renew our minds daily to make sure we don't fall into the world's traps. So, as we said before, we have to change our minds (repent), but we can't stop there. Why? Because if we change our minds and aren't transformed, we can change our minds again. From this point, in order for the full transformation to happen, we have to make sure that we are renewing our minds. Again, Romans 12:2 says, ***"And be not conformed to this world: but be ye transformed by the renewing of your mind, that ye may prove what is that good, and acceptable, and perfect, will of God."***

Romans 12:2 reminds me of that parable about the sower. 3 out of the 4 sowers weren't transformed, because their mind wasn't renewed. Matthew 13:19-22 says, ***"When any one heareth the Word of the Kingdom, and understandeth it not, then cometh the wicked one, and catcheth away that which was sown in his heart. This is he which received seed by the way side. But he that received the seed into stony places, the same is he that heareth the Word, and anon with joy receiveth it; Yet hath he not root in himself, but dureth for a while: for when tribulation or persecution ariseth because of the Word, by and by he is offended. He also that received seed among the thorns is he that heareth the Word; and the care of this world, and the deceitfulness of riches, choke the Word, and he becometh unfruitful."***

When we repent (change our mind) we need to get in the Word to come into the full knowledge of Christ. When we do, we will not only understand why we believe what we believe, but begin to live lives that reflect it. When we do this, the enemy can't take away the Word that was sown like he did with the sower who sowed his seed on the wayside. When we get rooted in God's Word, we aren't easily moved by persecution like the sower who sowed seed on stony ground. Our renewed mind will help us not be so easily persuaded to change back to those old ways of living because of the cares of the world and deceitful riches. We also won't be like the one sower who sowed his seed among thorns and have the Word choked out of us.

We will do what Paul told the church at Ephesus in Ephesians 4:22-24, ***"That ye put off concerning the former conversation the old man, which is corrupt according to the deceitful lusts; And be renewed in the spirit of your mind; And that ye put on the new man, which after God is created in righteousness and true holiness."*** How does that happen? Through righteousness and holiness! Keep in mind, I did not say perfection; I said righteousness, which means being in right standing with God, and holiness, which means being set apart. 2 Corinthians 5:21 says, ***"For He hath made Him to be sin for us, Who knew no sin; that we might be made the righteousness of God in Him."*** Remember, our righteousness doesn't come from us, but from what Christ did for us.

Our renewed mind doesn't allow us to look, talk, or think the way we did before. Why? Because we've been transformed by the Truth. This also reflects in our actions. For instance, if a person renewed their mind about eating healthier, what will we notice as a result of their renewed mind? Their actions will reflect their mind, which will produce the results of the changes they've made. The same with a spiritually renewed mind. The results will be noticeable to others because you will begin to look the way you think. I am not just talking about physical appearance either. I am also referring to what Colossians 3:10 says, ***"And have put on the new self, which is being renewed in knowledge after the image of its Creator."*** When our mind is renewed, we will look more like God's image! Wiki says, *"As a verb image is to represent symbolically."*

The more we behold His glory, the more His glory transforms us into His image or should I say re-symbols (resembles) His image. 2 Corinthians 3:18, ***"And we all, with unveiled face, beholding the glory of the Lord, are being transformed into the same image from one degree of glory to another. For this comes from the Lord Who is the Spirit."*** When people see us, they can't help but to see God in us because the glory transforms and covers us with God's image. So what do we have to renew our minds about? Romans 8:5-8 says, ***"For they that are after the flesh do mind the things of the flesh; but they that are after the Spirit the things of the Spirit. For to be carnally minded is death; but to be spiritually minded is life and peace. Because the carnal mind is enmity against God: for it is not subject to the law of God, neither indeed can***

be. So then they that are in the flesh cannot please God. We have to go from being carnal minded which produces death and be spiritually minded, which produces life and peace.

God is eternal and He made us in His image. Therefore, His will is not death for us, and it never was. Ezekiel 18:32 says, ***"For I take no pleasure in the death of anyone, declares the Sovereign Lord. Repent and live!"*** The initial goal, which is the fact that God's will (desired outcome) is not death, but life. Not just life, but eternal life. In order to have eternal life, the way that we thought prior to receiving Christ has to change. If our mindset is changed, then we would not live carnally like before. Instead, we would live a life that is according to the will of God. So, when I say a mind of Christ, that is the renewed mind that chooses the will of God, not the will of man. Why? Because the recipe in 1 John 2:17 tells us the desired results (God's will), ***"The world and its desires pass away, but whoever does the will of God lives forever."***

CHANGE AGENT: Help Change the Minds of Others:
We make "being in this world, but not of it" a difficult thing, even though we've been given an example. Hebrews 4:15 says, ***"For we have not an High Priest which cannot be touched with the feeling of our infirmities; but was in all points tempted like as we are, yet without sin."*** Jesus didn't adapt to the behaviors of this world just because He was in this world. Although He was human just like us, as long as He was here, He followed God's recipe to get the desired results. Again, Philippians 2:5-11 says, ***"Let this***

mind be in you, which was also in Christ Jesus: Who, being in the form of God, thought it not robbery to be equal with God: But made Himself of no reputation, and took upon Him the form of a servant, and was made in the likeness of men: And being found in fashion as a man, He humbled Himself, and became obedient unto death, even the death of the cross. Wherefore God also hath highly exalted Him, and given Him a Name which is above every name: That at the Name of Jesus every knee should bow, of things in heaven, and things in earth, and things under the earth; And that every tongue should confess that Jesus Christ is Lord, to the glory of God the Father."

Not only was it beneficial for Jesus to have the mindset that He did, but it was also beneficial for us. He taught us what type of mindset we needed to have, especially as believers! Before Paul described what type of mind they should have, he said how they should live. Philippians 2:1-4 says, ***"If there be therefore any consolation in Christ, if any comfort of love, if any fellowship of the Spirit, if any bowels and mercies, Fulfil ye my joy, that ye be likeminded, having the same love, being of one accord, of one mind. Let nothing be done through strife or vainglory; but in lowliness of mind let each esteem other better than themselves. Look not every man on his own things, but every man also on the things of others."*** He followed up by encouraging them that the same mind he told them to have was the same kind Jesus had.

Paul wasn't high minded, but had a mind to see that others were reconciled to God. In order for us to be change agents, our mind towards each other has to be a mind and heart that desires to see us all walk in the fullness of what God has promised us. We wouldn't have it if Christ didn't have that type of mind towards us. The only way we can have this mind is if we don't have a mind that pleases the flesh, but one that minds the things of the Spirit. Remember, Romans 8:5 says, ***"For they that are after the flesh do mind the things of the flesh; but they that are after the Spirit the things of the Spirit."*** Jesus came to reconcile us back to God. So in order for us to have that mind, we can't have the mind we had before that wants to please the flesh. We must have the mind of Christ because it is the mind that helps us to live a life pleasing to God! When we live like this, people will see the fruit that comes from our lives.

I've learned that most of the time, our impact is not in what we say but how we live. Paul told the church at Corinth in 1 Corinthians 11:1, ***"Be ye followers of me, even as I also am of Christ."*** As change agents, we live lives that model Christ, so that we lead others to do the same. This would be impossible without a renewed mind. More specifically, it wouldn't be possible without a renewed mind in Christ. When we as believers renew our minds, our lives reflect that change. From there, we should encourage others, through our lives as well as by the Word of God, to not only change their minds (repent), but to also be transformed by the renewing of their minds. This should perpetuate change with all we impact as well as the ones who will be impacted by those we impact as well.

Hebrews 10:24 says, ***"And let us consider one another to provoke unto love and to good works:".***

THE CONCLUSION Chapter 14.

Ecclesiastes 12:13 says, ***"Let us hear the conclusion of the whole matter: Fear God, and keep His commandments: for this is the whole duty of man."*** When I say, "You're the problem…", I am saying that because this was an honest conversation I had to have with myself. I blamed a lot of things and people for the undesired results I was getting, when all the while, I was the problem. That was the hardest, but most revelatory thing God showed me about myself. I never had a problem figuring out everyone else's problem, but I couldn't come to the same conclusion about my own. James 1:23-25 says, ***"For if any be a hearer of the Word, and not a doer, he is like unto a man beholding his natural face in a glass: For he beholdeth himself, and goeth his way, and straightway forgetteth what manner of man he was. But whoso looketh into the perfect law of liberty, and continueth therein, he being not a forgetful hearer, but a doer of the work, this man shall be blessed in his deed."***

Basically, I had the recipes all along, but I wasn't following any of them. Since I wasn't following the recipes, I didn't remember that the problem looked like my face that I saw in the mirror. If you choose in life not to do the recipe, that's your choice. However, when you begin blaming everything and everyone else for your results, you will always get those same results because you aren't addressing the problem. When you get to the point that God got me to and realize your problem is your inconsistency with the recipe, then you can begin to see different and desirable results in your life. For me, I had to learn that doing works wasn't the same as doing the Word. I never realized I was the problem because I thought what I was doing was right. My works became the whole foundation of my "relationship" with God. Since my foundation was built on what I had to do, my relationship with God was a very unstable construct.

The reason my relationship with God was unstable was because I never accepted what Jesus did for me as enough. I would always unconsciously and sometimes consciously try to work for God's love and approval. Ephesians 2:8-9 says, ***"For by grace are ye saved through faith; and that not of yourselves: it is the gift of God: Not of works, lest any man should boast."*** If this was my mindset, what happened when I didn't get it right or didn't work hard enough to my standards? I would create this imaginary distance between God and me because of my disappointment in what I couldn't do. Although I wanted to get to God by my works, I also understood that God was gracious. I would tell people about the incredible, free grace and love of God all the time. However, I wouldn't receive it for myself. Jesus warned against this to His disciples because the religious leaders around that time were trying to gain access to God through what they were doing instead of what Jesus would do for them.

It made no sense to work for what was free, so why was I doing it? Well, it was because I didn't fully follow Jesus' recipe. As long as I was doing it my way, I could not have a relationship with God as He desired for us. My behavior meant that God and I weren't in a relationship, but in a business partnership. Jesus didn't want me in business with Him, because that meant we had equal responsibility. However, Jesus didn't ask me to die for Him or anyone in order for me to be saved. Jesus died for us once and for all. 2 Timothy 1:9 says, ***"Who hath saved us, and called us with an holy calling, not according to our works, but according to His own purpose and grace, which was given us in Christ Jesus before the world began,"***. Even if Jesus and I were in business together, the only reason that business wouldn't work, was because I wouldn't let God work in or on it.

Being a doer of God's Word (following His recipe) does not mean I had to do things in my own strength. The truth is that it wasn't just what I was doing, but also what I wasn't doing. This may still sound like work, but it's not. Works are what you're using to gain His approval or His love. However, doing what He said to do is allowing His love to be expressed to you and through you, to others. No matter how strong we may think we are, we couldn't even do God's will if He doesn't work in us to do it. Philippians 2:13 says, ***"For it is God which worketh in you both to will and to do of His good pleasure."*** Contrary to what I believed, I still wasn't doing anything in and of myself. I still needed God to empower me for whatever I was doing, especially His will! I had to learn that God will not give us instructions to do His will without also empowering us to do it!

I still have to remind myself that we aren't justified by what we do, but by our belief that Jesus already did it for us. Galatians 2:16 says, ***"Knowing that a man is not justified by the works of the law, but by the faith of Jesus Christ, even we have believed in Jesus Christ, that we might be justified by the faith of Christ, and not by the works of the law: for by the works of the law shall no flesh be justified."*** I can only speak for myself, that the things I was doing contrary to His Word (recipe) were Law inspired. There's nothing wrong with the Law, except I was trying to be justified by doing it. For those not following the Word (recipe), you could simply be doing what you want to and none of what He's telling you to do. Whatever the case may be, when we aren't following the recipe, we have become our only problem. In order for us to find the solution, we have to get rid of what we want to do, and only do what He has asked us to do. This may feel like you're losing yourself, but isn't that the point?

Matthew 16:24-25 says, ***"Then said Jesus unto His disciples, If any man will come after Me, let him deny himself, and take up his cross, and follow Me. For whosoever will save his life shall lose it: and whosoever will lose his life for My sake shall find it."*** I know this scripture can be used to address those who chase after worldly things instead of following Jesus, but I believe God revealed another point that can be made here. Jesus didn't just tell His disciples to follow Him as in where He would journey. He also told them to follow after His ways. Unfortunately, you can't hold onto God's way, without letting go of your way. In order to fully submit to His way, we have to totally let go of ours. Paul says in Philippians 3:13-14, ***"Brethren, I count not myself to have apprehended: but this one thing I do, forgetting those things which are behind, and reaching forth unto those things which are before, I press toward the mark for the prize of the high calling of God in Christ Jesus."***

Denying yourself isn't just fasting, but it is also about denying your will/way. Letting go of who you were is also a form of denying yourself. If we are going to get the desired results, we are going to have to let go of how we want to do things and grab onto our new identity in Christ with both hands. I had to learn the hard way, but glory to God, I learned, and I am still learning! I still have to work on not working because I still have areas that I try to work for God's love. However, I am learning to accept the grace of God. Romans 11:6 says, ***"And if by grace, then is it no more of works: otherwise grace is no more grace. But if it be of works, then it is no more grace: otherwise work is no more work."*** As I am typing right now, I made a mistake with a word. I didn't initially notice it at first, but autocorrect did. That's not works, but grace. How about when I do catch my mistakes and correct them, that is also grace that God allowed me to catch the error the autocorrect didn't and still correct it.

God's grace and love is that He either corrects or He shows us the problem and the solution as to how to correct it. We can't take responsibility for any of it. No matter how hard you work to try to be right, you could never do it on your own. I don't think we really realize how much of a grace it is to even know that you have a problem to correct. Knowing it is one grace and correcting it is another. Neither came from your works, but from your obedience. Some people think God has given them a grace to identify and correct problems with other people and not themselves. You can't correct the problem in your life by finding the problems in others. Matthew 7:3-5 says, ***"And why beholdest thou the mote that is in thy brother's eye, but considerest not the beam that is in thine own eye? Or how wilt thou say to thy brother, Let me pull out the mote out of thine eye; and, behold, a beam is in thine own eye? Thou hypocrite, first cast out the beam out of thine own eye; and then shalt thou see clearly to cast out the mote out of thy brother's eye."*** You first recognize the problems in our own lives and then and only then will you be able to help others to see and find solutions to their problems. I don't want us to leave each other without asking God to help us all be the best versions of ourselves.

Pray with me:

Dear Lord,
I pray that You give us a new heart to desire Your way.
Right perspective to see Your Word as the Light unto our path.
New ears to hear the Holy Spirit's leading us on the right path.
New eyes to see that Your Word as the solution.
The diligence to apply Your Word to our lives.
The obedience to follow Your Word and Your Way.
In Jesus' Name, Amen!

Don't worry about having the problem, just know God has given us everything that we need to correct the problem. You might have been the problem, but His Word has the recipe for the solution. Let's give it another try.. This time, let's follow the recipe (His Word). Glory to God in advance!

Matthew 7:24-25 says, ***"Therefore whosoever heareth these sayings of Mine, and doeth them, I will liken him unto a wise man, which built his house upon a rock: And the rain descended, and the floods came, and the winds blew, and beat upon that house; and it fell not: for it was founded upon a rock."***

TO...

My daughter, Gabrielle Lyric. Angelic Messenger. You are the first reason I was blessed to be called mom. For a couple of years, it was just you, but I am so grateful that I not only get to see you as my daughter, but also as an amazing big sister. You are the artist I wish I could've been. Never question who God has called you to be and never let this world make you into who you're not. The Holy Spirit will speak to you more and more the closer you get to Him. Those Words are from God and you are the deliverer of that message. Keep speaking His Words!

My daughter, Paisley Elle. Church. My sweet baby girl. You remind me so much of myself, in that you are sweet, gentle, and kind. However, you have something that I never had when I was younger, boldness. You have a mind of your own, which is a mind of Christ. This is why no one can make you do or say what the Holy Spirit doesn't agree with. Continue to stand up for what is right, regardless of how unpopular it is. You are truly made in the image of God. Paisley, your creative ability is beyond imagination, so keep creating!

My son, Judah Arrows. Praiser. God gave us your name first, but I didn't know I would have to wait 3 years to meet you. It was definitely worth the wait! You are one of the most remarkable young men I have ever met. I pray that you exceed all expectations as a man! Although your intellect and athleticism is unmatched, remember that there's a praise on the inside of you that will never go out. Don't try to quench it! Keep praising Him! Like 1 Timothy

4:12 said, don't let anyone look down on you for your youth, but set the example!

The **three** of you are so inspiring to me. I pray that you always use what I do as your stepping stone and not as your ceiling. May you all always have an amazing balance of confidence and humility in the gifts God has blessed you with! I love you all dearly, but God loves you more!

Mom, I thank God for you for being the best at what you do and so cool and so jazzy while doing it. Live only for His purpose/glory! And as it pertains to your gift… God is not through with you yet! May God redeem the time and bless your latter to be greater than your former!

Rashada, big sister, you are evidence of God's faithfulness! Girl, you're alive to see this! ALL GLORY TO GOD! However, we both know the real reason He kept you is for the purpose He created you for! By now you've realized what that purpose is so just continue living according to it! I give God all the glory that I have my teammate back, but this time for the Kingdom of God!

Sedonn, big bro. You're a force for the Kingdom of God! I love when we talk about a scripture we read, the sermon we heard or a passionate conversation about the End Times. I can't wait for the world to hear the Word of God from you the way I do! It's powerful! All glory to God! I pray you continue to minister and speak with boldness!

Jonathan, lil bro, I think you are one of the strongest people I know! I pray that you realize not only your potential, but the purpose God created you for! I know that you have been set apart for God's glory, and I pray that people will overcome by the Blood of the Lamb and the word of your testimony! In Jesus Name, Amen!

Gary, **Christy**, **Tracey**, **Robert**, **Shaina**, and **Shauri**, God was intentional about you and the gift He has given to you! I pray you not only live for Him and His glory, but also fulfill the purpose that He created you for! I am grateful for any moments we've shared. They haven't gone unnoticed. For the memories we have yet to share, I look forward to them. And **Joyce**, Lord willing we get a chance to meet. **Dad**, I haven't forgotten you and I miss you dearly! I almost said I hate you didn't get to see this, but honestly, I don't because I know you're getting to see the fullness of God's glory! What better sight than that?! Oh and God is still answering your prayers in the earth! All glory to God! **Pastor Green** and **Mrs. Dee**, May God bless you both without limits for all of your sacrifices and according to Isa. 1:19, may you both eat the good of the land because of your willingness and obedience to God! All glory to God! **Family**, **Friends**, and **Loved Ones**, God created each of you with a specific purpose. Ask God what it is, live according to it, and may the world be blessed by it!

If I don't say anything else, let me say to those reading this, that if you haven't accepted Jesus Christ as Your Lord and Savior, now is the time to do it. Romans 10:9 (NKJV) says, ***"that if you confess with your mouth the Lord Jesus and believe in your heart that God has raised Him from the dead, you will be saved."*** If you prayed this prayer, welcome to the family of God. If you haven't already, make that your number 1 priority so we can all link in eternity!

Thank You God for them all and for it all! I am beyond grateful to You! As always, "ALL GLORY TO GOD!"

Made in the USA
Coppell, TX
21 June 2026

82980822R00173